# PENNSYLVANIA DAY TRIPS

LORI LITCHMAN

**Safety Note** Pennsylvania is home to a variety of potentially dangerous animals, including venomous snakes, as well as natural hazards, such as temperature extremes, sudden flash floods, and cliffs and dropoffs. Always heed posted safety warnings, take commonsense safety precautions, and remain aware of your surroundings. You're responsible for your own safety.

Editor: Andrew Mollenkof
Cover and book design: Hilary Harkness
Proofreader: Emily Beaumont
Typography: Karla Linder
Maps: Steve Jones
Indexer: Potomac Indexing, LLC
Front cover photos: Shofuso Japanese House: Zachary Chung Pun/shutterstock.com; asphalt: Irina Gutyryak/shutterstock.com; liberty bell: PCAStudio-1/shutterstock.com
Back cover photos: Fallingwater: WillAshely/shutterstock.com; Independence Hall: Sean Pavone/shutterstock
Photo credits on page 142
ADK branding background on page 144 by chyworks/Shutterstock.com

10 9 8 7 6 5 4 3 2 1
**Pennsylvania Day Trips by Theme**
First Edition 2025

Published by Adventure Publications
An imprint of AdventureKEEN
310 Garfield Street South
Cambridge, Minnesota 55008
(800) 678-7006
adventurepublications.net

Printed in China
Library of Congress Control Number: 2025945439
ISBN 978-1-64755-495-8 (pbk.); 978-1-64755-496-5 (ebook)

**Disclaimer** Please note that travel information changes under the impact of many factors that influence the travel industry. We therefore suggest that you call ahead for confirmation when making your travel plans. Every effort has been made to ensure the accuracy of information throughout this book, and the contents of this publication are believed to be correct at the time of printing. Nevertheless, the publishers cannot accept responsibility for errors or omissions, for changes in details given in this guide, or for the consequences of any reliance on the information provided by the same. Assessments of attractions and so forth are based upon the author's own experiences; therefore, descriptions given in this guide necessarily contain an element of subjective opinion, which may not reflect the publisher's opinion or dictate a reader's own experience on another occasion.

To the children of Pennsylvania. May you explore new places, play outside, and learn about our shared history.


## ACKNOWLEDGMENTS

I'm always grateful to Tim Jackson, who first connected me to AdventureKEEN. Thanks to Senior Acquisitions Editor Brett Ortler. Special shout-out to those who came along on research trips—Marnie, Michelle, & Jen K. Much love to my husband, Dave Tavani.


## AUTHOR'S NOTE

*Pennsylvania Day Trips* is my best effort to harness all of the amazing places to visit in my great home state and compile them all in one place. Sadly, there are places and spaces I had to leave out because there just wasn't room. I also tried to geographically cover the entire state, which was quite a feat considering that Pennsylvania is 46,000 square miles.

I believe everyone is entitled to enjoy these places in a way that is safe and comfortable, so I've included information regarding accessibility at these points of interest. Some places in the book are outdoors with uneven surfaces, and a number of historic spots have inaccessible areas with architecture that does not meet modern accessibility standards. I was delighted to find that many places have resources for those with sight and hearing concerns or sensory challenges.

While I've included basic accessibility information, I also encourage you to reach out directly anywhere you aren't sure meets your accessibility needs. Many of these locations say on their websites or over email that even if their space has limitations, they will do their best to accommodate everyone. Additionally, many museums participate in the "Museums for All" program, offering discounted and/or free entrance for those who receive food assistance benefits. Similarly, many gardens that charge fees also offer discounted rates for ACCESS cardholders. Check websites to find out more.

## FREE DAY TRIPS

Allegheny National Forest

Allentown Art Museum

The August Wilson African American Cultural Center

Bartram's Garden

Bear Creek Preserve

Buttermilk Falls

Caledonia State Park

Cherry Springs State Park

Cherry Valley National Wildlife Refuge

Cook Forest State Park

Delaware Water Gap National Recreation Area

The Demuth Museum

D.G. Yuengling & Sons, Inc.

Dingmans Falls

The Discovery Center

Edgar Allan Poe National Historic Site

Elk Country Visitor Center

Erie National Wildlife Refuge

Falls Trail at Ricketts Glen State Park

Flight 93 National Memorial

Fort Necessity

The Frick Pittsburgh Museum & Gardens

Goodell Gardens & Homestead

Great Allegheny Passage

Hickory Run State Park Boulder Field

H.O. Smith Botanic Gardens & Arboretum at Penn State University

Institute of Contemporary Art University of Pennsylvania

Jenkins Arboretum & Gardens

John F. Kennedy Plaza (LOVE Park)

John Heinz National Wildlife Refuge

Knoebels Amusement Park

Lancaster Museum of Art

Laurel Hill East & West

Leonard Harrison State Park

Linvilla Orchards

Mcconells Mill State Park

Middle Creek Wildlife Management Area

Moka Origins

Mt. Airy Orchards

Ned Smith Center for Nature & Art

Ohiopyle State Park

Oil Creek State Park

Palmer Museum of Art

Peace Valley Nature Center

The Pennsylvania State Capital
Pine Grove Furnace State Park
Powdermill Nature Reserve
Presque Isle State Park
Promised Land State Park
Raymondskill Falls
Raystown Lake
Ridley Creek State Park
Ringing Rocks County Park
Rocky Statue
Science History Institute Museum & Library
Seven Tubs Recreation Area
Shaver's Creek Environmental Center
Smith Memorial Playground
Steamtown
Stoneleigh
U.S. Mint
Valley Forge National Historic Park
Wagner Free Institute of Science
Wissahickon Valley Park
World's End State Park

# MAP 1

## EASTERN PENNSYLVANIA

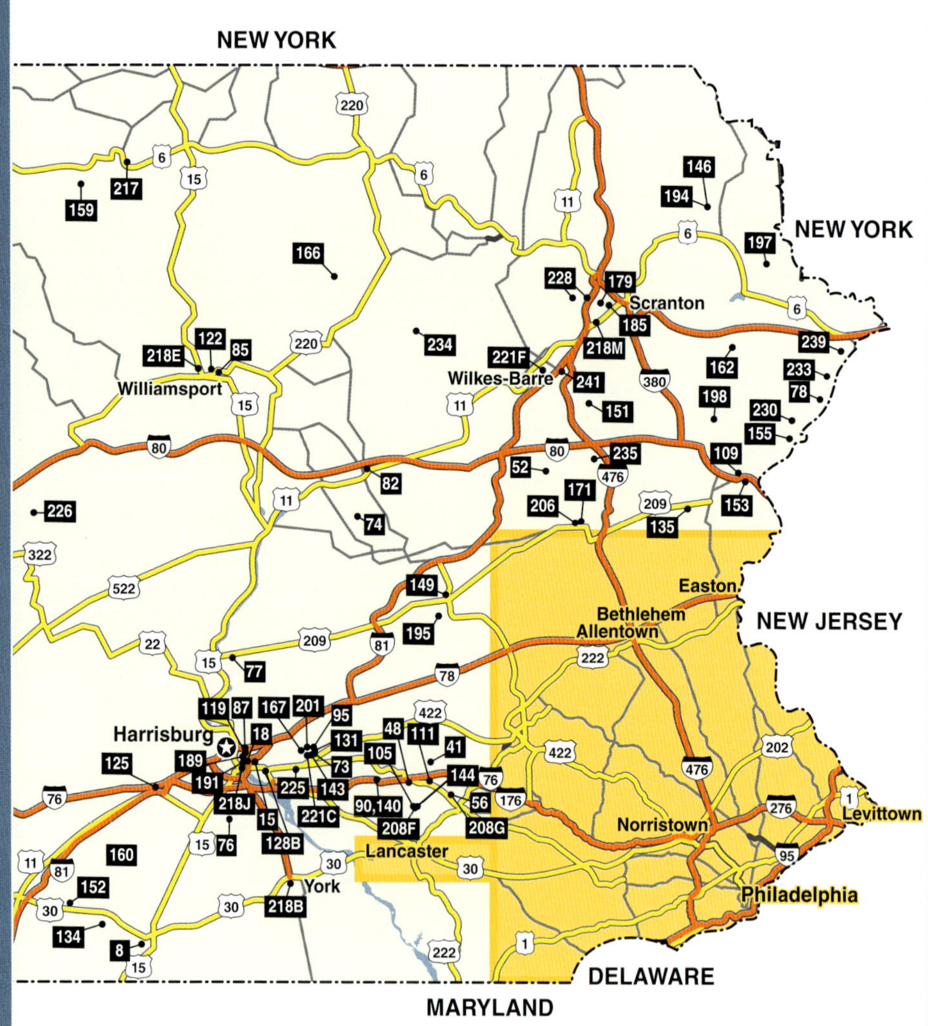

# CONTENTS

MAP 1 MAP 2 MAP 3 MAP 4 MAP 5

# MAP 2

## WESTERN PENNSYLVANIA

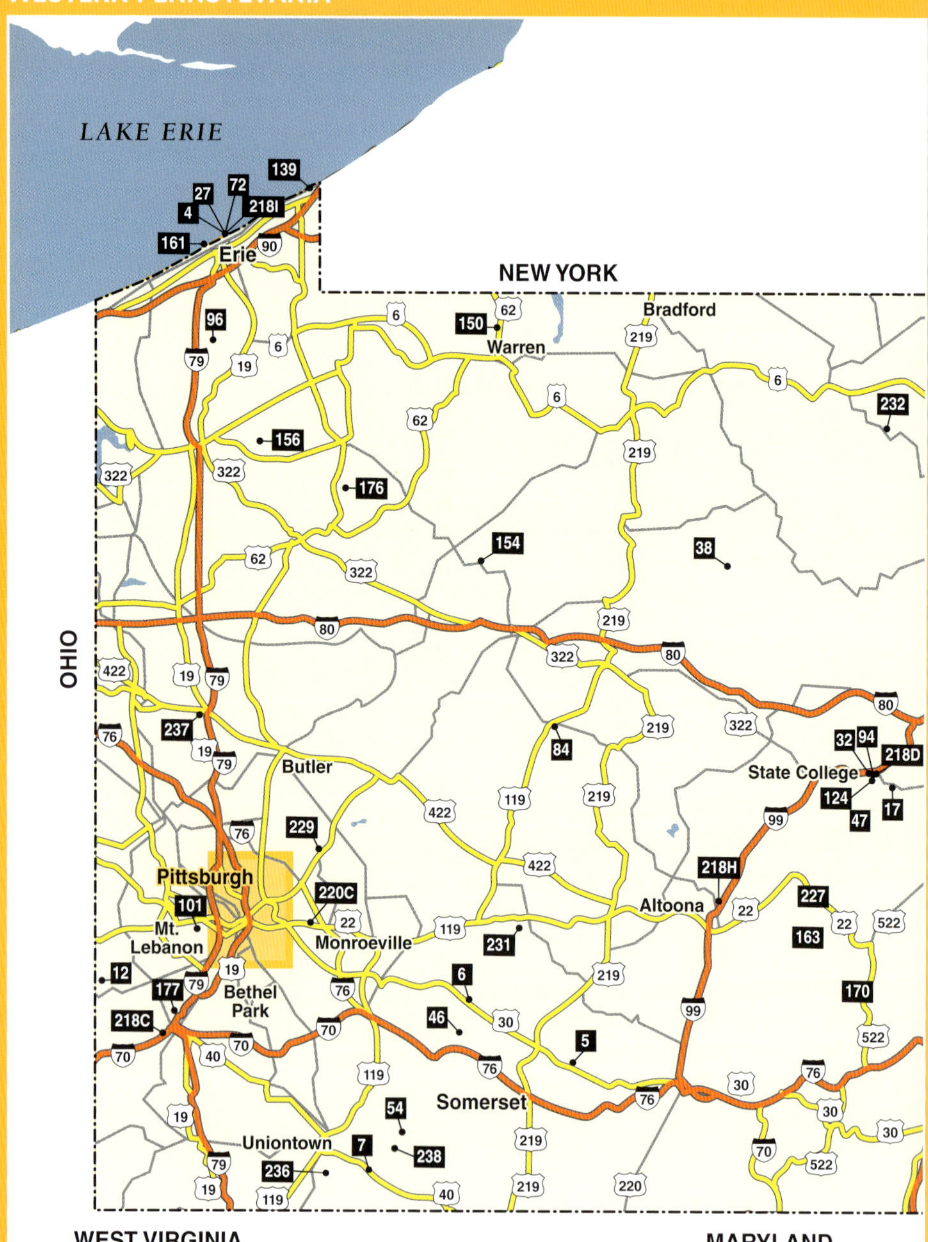

# CONTENTS

MAP 1 MAP 2 MAP 3 MAP 4 MAP 5

## MAP 3

# PITTSBURGH

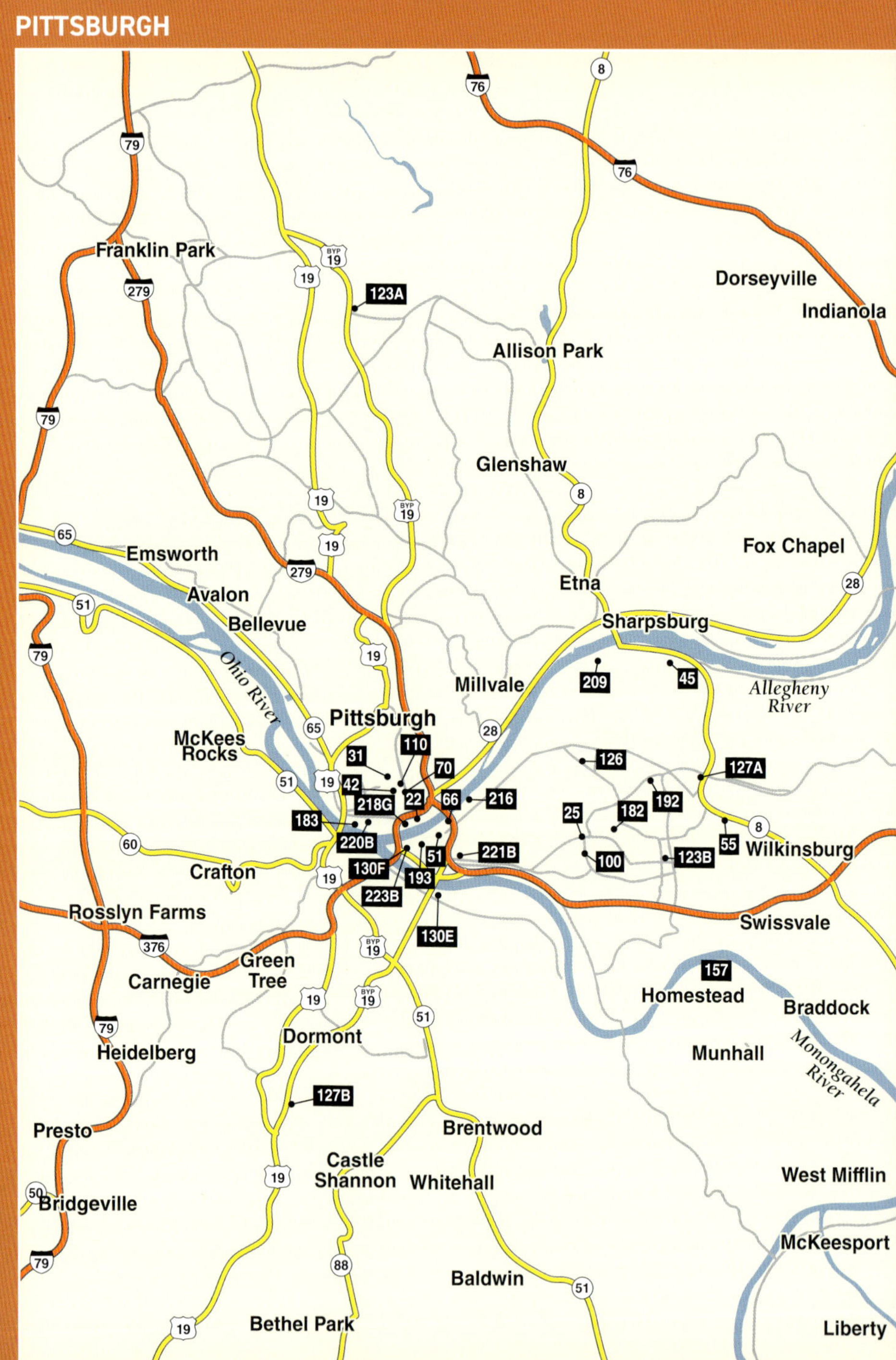

# CONTENTS

MAP 1 MAP 2 MAP 3 MAP 4 MAP 5

# MAP 4

## PHILADELPHIA

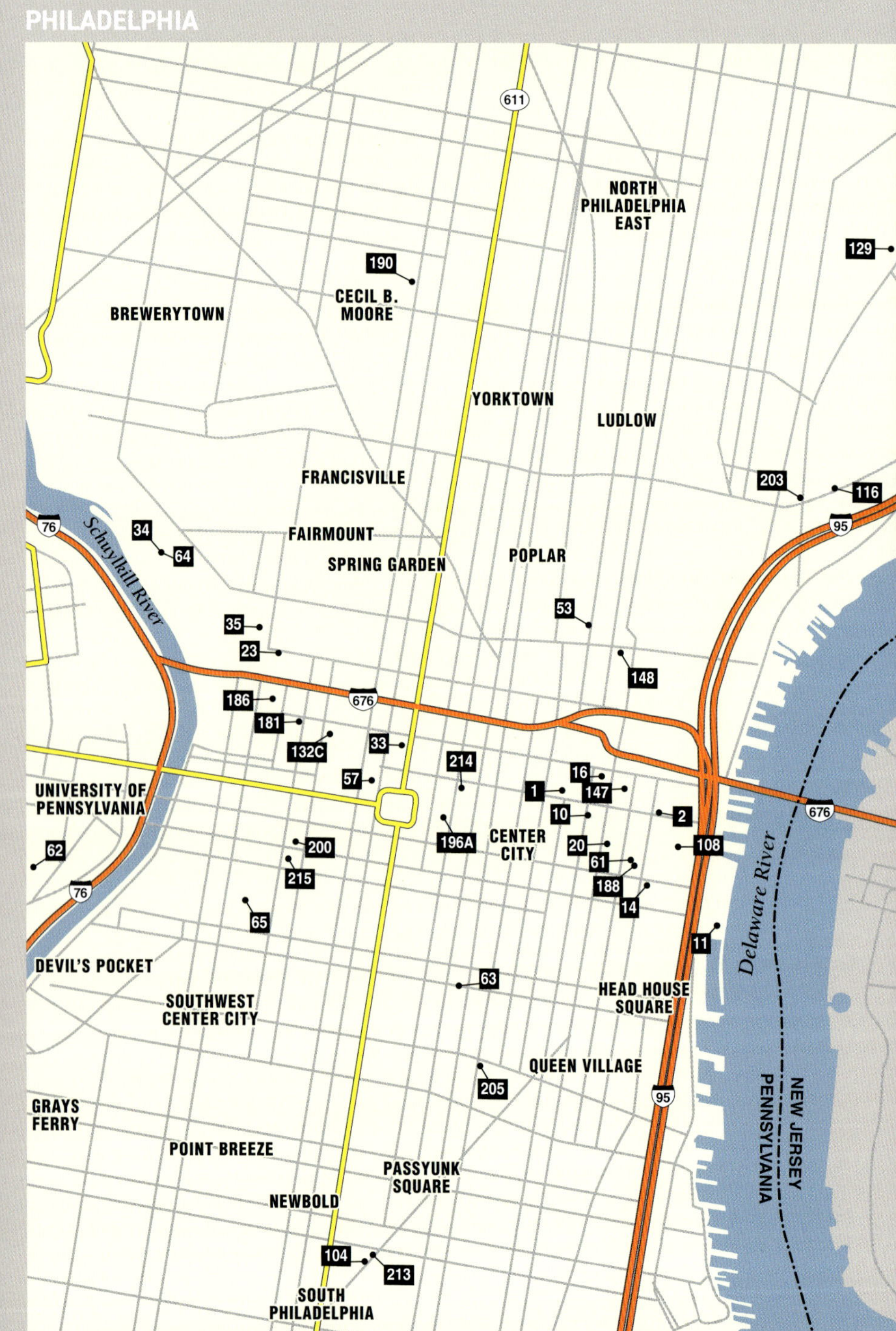

## CONTENTS

■ MAP 1 ■ MAP 2 ■ MAP 3 ■ MAP 4 ■ MAP 5

## MAP 5

## GREATER PHILADELPHIA AND LANCASTER AREAS

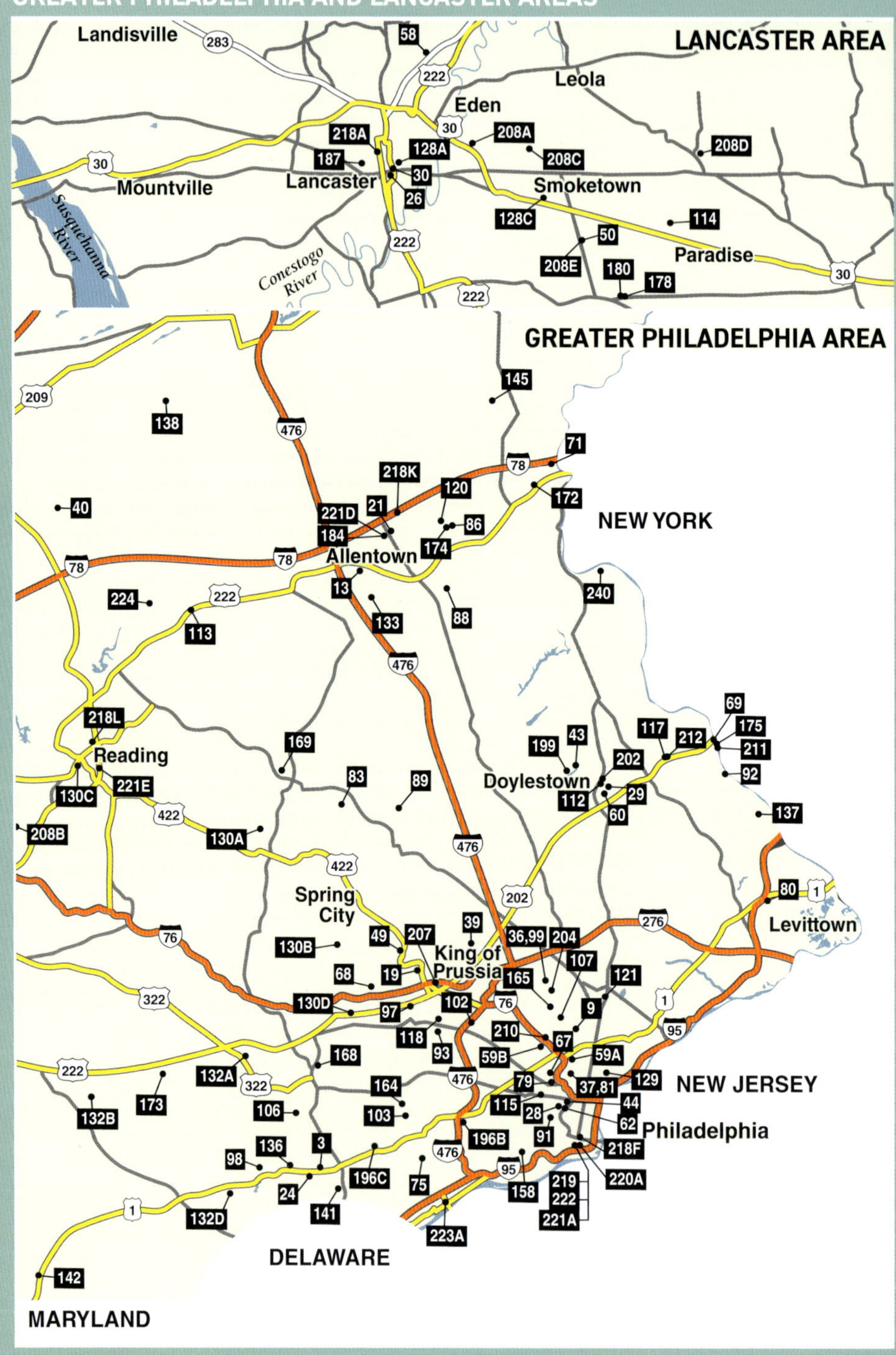

# CONTENTS

MAP 1 MAP 2 MAP 3 MAP 4 MAP 5

MCCONNELLS MILLS RED COVERED BRIDGE

MILKY WAY GALAXY FROM CHERRY SPRINGS STATE PARK

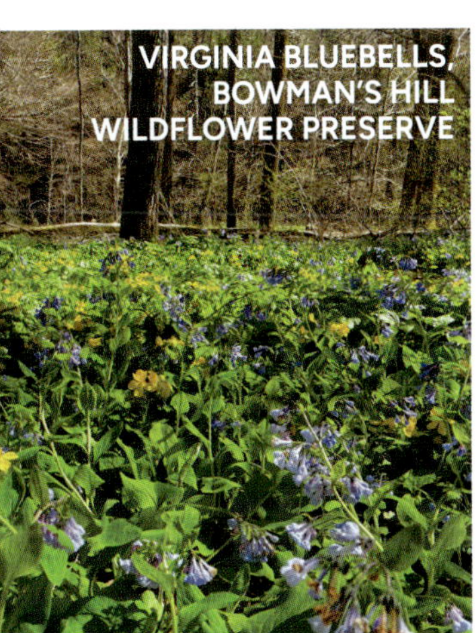

VIRGINIA BLUEBELLS, BOWMAN'S HILL WILDFLOWER PRESERVE

MAGIC GARDENS STAIRS

# INTRODUCTION

Welcome to *Pennsylvania Day Trips!* This book is your one-stop shop for planning travel in Pennsylvania that you can do in a day. The book is arranged thematically, so I encourage you to first look for places that meet your interests, and then refer to the map to see what else is nearby. I've occasionally offered suggestions of places that are near one another.

I began my research by reading the Economic Impact of Pennsylvania's Travel and Tourism Industry Report. Millions visit every year, supporting the livelihoods of hundreds of thousands of state residents. I discovered that visitors tend to visit Philadelphia the most, followed by Pennsylvania Dutch Country, Pittsburgh, and then the Pocono Mountains region. As I began to gather locations to include, I started with those four regions, then expanded out to include the entire state because there are hidden treasures in every pocket of Pennsylvania.

If you've never visited the state before, you are in for a real treat. We've got history like no other place in the country, peaceful yet rugged forests and outdoor spaces, cities bursting with art and culture, and food that will make you hunger for more. Pennsylvania is full of heartfelt people who are welcoming and friendly. I've lived in Philadelphia for more than three decades; our sports fans are passionate to say the least. Yet I have found some of the friendliest people I've ever met in Philly, despite its sometimes gruff reputation. Pennsylvanians love to share our history and gorgeous spaces with newcomers. We are proud of our past and hopeful for our future. If you live here or have visited before, you already know all of this information, but I hope you'll find some new destinations in this book to add to your travel itinerary. I guarantee you won't be disappointed. In 2024, Governor Josh Shapiro dubbed Pennsylvania "The Great American Getaway." I couldn't agree more. So, gather your family and friends and get ready to check out all that Pennsylvania has to offer. We can't wait to meet you.

*WE THE PEOPLE* EXHIBIT AT THE NATIONAL CONSTITUTION CENTER, PHILADELPHIA

# America was born in Pennsylvania.

The founding fathers gathered in Philadelphia to craft the Declaration of Independence and, later, the U.S. Constitution. Pennsylvania also has numerous historic battlefields you can visit. The state was thrust into the spotlight during one of our nation's saddest days, September 11, 2001, when a hijacked airplane crashed in a field in Western Pennsylvania. The state is also home to an archaeological site that changed everything we had known about humans on this continent. If you are a history buff, you will love these sites. If you aren't, visiting these sites will surely convert you.

# Welcome to AMERICAN HISTORY

# *Find out more about* AMERICAN HISTORY

## AFRICAN AMERICAN MUSEUM IN PHILADELPHIA

**701 Arch Street**
**Philadelphia, PA 19106; 215-574-0380**
**aampmuseum.org**
***Wheelchair accessible.***

The African American Museum in Philadelphia, a Smithsonian affiliate, is located in the city's historic district, steps away from Independence Hall. It tells the story of the African American experience in Philadelphia and the nation from colonial to modern times. You'll learn about African American heritage and history throughout the museum's four galleries, including arts, science, sports, politics, and civil rights. The permanent exhibit, *Audacious Freedom: African Americans in Philadelphia 1776–1876*, is interactive and dynamic. There's also a Children's Corner with hands-on activities and installations for the little ones. The museum regularly changes exhibits, so check the website before your visit.

## 2 BETSY ROSS HOUSE

**239 Arch Street**
**Philadelphia, PA 19106; 215-629-4026**
**historicphiladelphia.org/betsy-ross-house/**
***Partial wheelchair accessibility. First floor is accessible and an audio/photo tour is available for those with mobility issues in lieu of touring the historic home.***

Nestled in the historic Old City neighborhood of Philadelphia, you'll find the Betsy Ross House. The historic home is just a few blocks away from Independence Hall and makes a great addition to a day trip. The house museum is fairly small, but it is packed with information and artifacts. Betsy is credited with stitching the first American flag. You may even get to meet Betsy herself, at work in her upholstery business. The courtyard outside the Betsy Ross House has a number of tables and makes for a great lunch spot if the weather is nice. You can also visit Betsy's and her third husband's graves in the courtyard. You can pay a bit extra for an audio tour or take the self-guided route and read the info along the way.

## 3 BRANDYWINE BATTLEFIELD PARK

**1491 Baltimore Pike**
**Chadds Ford PA, 19317; 610-459–3342**
**brandywinebattlefield.org**
***Wheelchair accessible.***

Brandywine Battlefield is a huge site, stretching 50 square miles between Chester and Delaware Counties. It's the site of "the largest single-day land battle of the American Revolution." The address above will take you to the visitor center, where you can plan out your day. There's an 18-minute film if you'd like to learn more about the history of the battle and available tours of Washington's headquarters. The field portion of the site offers a nice walking trail where you can learn more about the battle and visit some historic buildings, such as an icehouse, a spring house, and a blacksmith's shop. You'll get a feel for what life was like during this pivotal time in American history.

## 4 ERIE MARITIME MUSEUM

150 East Front Street
Erie, PA 16507; 814-452-2744
eriemaritimemuseum.org
*Museum is wheelchair accessible, but the ship is not.*

The Erie Maritime Museum is located on the shores of Lake Erie and is the home port of the *US Brig Niagara*. The ship is a replica of the one used in the Battle of Lake Erie, and when it's open, visitors can tour and go for a sail. As of the publication of this book, the iconic tall ship is undergoing years-long maintenance and upgrades and is slated to return to sailing in 2026. In the meantime, visitors can visit the museum to learn the stories of the ship and maritime history along the shores of the Great Lake. Exhibits also teach all about the Battle of 1812 and how ships were used in battle in early American history.

## 5 FLIGHT 93 NATIONAL MEMORIAL FREE

6424 Lincoln Highway
Stoystown, PA 15563; 814-893-6322
nps.gov/flni
*Fully accessible.*

September 11, 2001, was one of the most devastating days in American history, with more than 3,000 lives lost in the terrorist attacks. Flight 93 crashed in a field in Western Pennsylvania, thrusting this part of rural Pennsylvania into the spotlight as the nation mourned. The Flight 93 Memorial is a solemn place with gut-wrenching exhibits in the visitor center. I was not the only person crying on a recent visit, so prepare yourself for the experience if you go. The site is stunningly peaceful and calm, with walking trails, an overlook, and a public sculpture called *The Tower of Voices*. The sculpture is 93 feet tall and has 40 wind chimes, one for each passenger or crew member lost that day.

## 6 FORT LIGONIER

200 South Market Street
Ligonier, PA 15658; 724-238-9701
fortligonier.org
*Partial accessibility. Museum and education center are wheelchair accessible, as are paved paths on the grounds. Historic buildings are not wheelchair accessible.*

Fort Ligonier was once the home base of British army soldiers in the 1700s. It was at this spot that the British fought against the French and Indigenous peoples in what would become known as the French and Indian War. The fort has been reconstructed to mimic the original site. The site really comes alive in the summer and autumn, featuring regular living history programming with reenactments and educational programming about life in the 18th century. The museum features art exhibits, historic artifacts, and relics discovered in archaeological digs on-site. Nearby Fort Necessity, which is about an hour's drive, might also make a good history-focused day trip.

## 7 FORT NECESSITY FREE

3 Washington Parkway
Farmington, PA 15437; 724-329-5805
nps.gov/fone
*Mostly wheelchair accessible. 2nd floor of Mount Washington Tavern not accessible.*

The French and Indian War pitted the British against the united French and native peoples. Early in the conflict, a young General George Washington prepared British forces for war. His troops built Fort Necessity, although they never planned to battle at this site. All that would change on July 3, 1754, when the British were attacked and forced to battle out of necessity. It would be the first action of what evolved into the French and Indian War. You can see the reconstructed barracks and cabin and explore the grounds, which include 5 miles of hiking trails. Summer months often feature tours, talks, and historic firearms demos. The National Park Service manages the site, located about 70 miles south of Pittsburgh.

## 8 GETTYSBURG NATIONAL MILITARY PARK

**1195 Baltimore Pike**
**Gettysburg, PA 17325; 717-334-1124**
**nps.gov/gett**
***Wheelchair accessible.***

Gettysburg National Military Park is a National Historic Site commemorating the bloodiest battle of the Civil War. It was a turning point in the war and the site of Abraham Lincoln's famed *Gettysburg Address*. To see everything at the 6,000-acre site, it's best to plan ahead; rangers recommend about four to six hours to explore. Start at the visitor center where you can grab a copy of the *Today in the Park* guidebook. There's also the museum, the expansive battlefield, and the national cemetery, which is the final resting place of fallen soldiers, and the site where Lincoln gave his famous speech. You have several options for tours, including a ranger-led guided tour, bus tours, self-guided car tours, and audio tours.

## 9 HISTORIC GERMANTOWN

**5501 Germantown Avenue**
**Philadelphia, PA 19144; 215-844-1683**
**historicgermantownpa.org**
***Accessibility varies by site. Check before your visit.***

Historic Germantown is a unique destination because it's a consortium of 19 separate historic homes, museums, burial grounds, and outdoor spaces. The best way to visit is to either start at the Germantown Historical Society to grab a map, or plan ahead using the website. Several of the historic spots are within walking distance, while others require car or bus travel. There's so much history in this neighborhood, including the Germantown White House, where George Washington stayed during the yellow fever epidemic of 1793. There's also Cliveden, the site of the Battle of Germantown; the Johnson House, a stop on the Underground Railroad; Rittenhousetown, a historic papermill in Wissahickon Valley Park (see page 86); Stenton, the historic home of James Logan; Wyck, home to one of the oldest rose gardens in the country; and Historic Fair Hill Burial Ground, the final resting place for abolitionists Robert Purvis and Lucretia Mott. Each site in the consortium offers its own programming. Regarding timing, Cliveden hosts a commemorative event each year in October around the anniversary of the Battle of Germantown, and Wyck's roses usually bloom in May.

## 10 INDEPENDENCE NATIONAL HISTORICAL PARK

**599 Market Street**
**Philadelphia PA 19106; 215-965-2305**
**nps.gov/inde**
***Fully accessible.***

Independence National Historical Park is one of the most popular destinations in Philadelphia and the country. It's where you can visit the room where it happened (if you are a *Hamilton* fan), and the Liberty Bell. Independence Hall is where both the Declaration of Independence and the U.S. Constitution were signed. Most of the time, you'll need to reserve a ticket to tour the building. There are open hours in the early morning and during winter months for self-guided tours. Otherwise, you can reserve tickets up to 30 days ahead of time. Day-before tickets open up daily at 5 p.m. But don't fret if you don't have a ticket. Show up and see if they can squeeze you in. You may have to wait a bit until there's space. No tickets are needed to see the Liberty Bell, but you'll have to go through security screening to see either site. There's also a fantastic visitor center with great exhibits. And if you want to spend the entire day exploring this part of Philadelphia, plan ahead and try to pack in some other spots. Close to Independence Hall you can find the National Constitution Center (see pages 9–10), the Museum of the American Revolution (see next page), the Betsy Ross House (see page 5), the National Liberty Museum (see page 35), the Science History Institute Museum & Library (see page 100), the African American Museum in Philadelphia (see page 5), the Weitzman National Museum of American Jewish History (see page 11), and Independence Seaport Museum (see page 8).

## 11 INDEPENDENCE SEAPORT MUSEUM

**211 South Columbus Boulevard**
**Philadelphia, PA 19106; 215-413-8655**
**phillyseaport.org**
***Museum is wheelchair accessible. Ships are not accessible.***

If you are drawn to water and ships, the Independence Seaport Museum will make a great day trip location for you. The museum tells the stories of Philadelphia's maritime history and features two ships. The *Olympia* is an 18th-century ship that saw active duty in the Spanish-American War, and visitors can explore it via self-guided or guided tour. Visitors can also take a guided tour of the *Becuna,* a WWII-era submarine that is the only one of its kind. If you decide to visit in the summer months and want to get out on the water, you can rent paddle boats or kayaks through Paddle Penn's Landing. The museum is located on the Delaware River waterfront, not far from Independence Hall (see previous).

## 12 MEADOWCROFT ROCK SHELTER & HISTORIC VILLAGE

**401 Meadowcroft Road**
**Avella, PA 15312; 724-587-3412**
**heinzhistorycenter.org/visit/meadowcroft**
***Partial wheelchair accessibility. Visitors center is accessible. The shelter is not, but guests with mobility issues can request a viewing of the video at the visitor center.***

Meadowcroft Rock Shelter & Historic Village is such a unique site, one of my favorites I discovered while writing this book. It's the site of an archaeological dig, which might sound boring until you learn that the dig uncovered evidence that changed everything historians thought they knew about the history of humans in North America. Before the dig, the belief was that humans came to the continent about 13,000 years ago. But discoveries at Meadowcroft produced evidence of human habitation from 19,000 years ago. You can see the actual site and watch a video about the discovery. There's also a cool historic village where you can learn about how early humans lived and see some living history programming. The Senator John Heinz History Center (page 37) manages the site.

## 13 MUSEUM OF INDIAN CULTURE

**2825 Fish Hatchery Road**
**Allentown, PA 18103; 610-797-2121**
**museumofindianculture.org**
***Contact before visiting to discuss accessibility needs.***

The Museum of Indian Culture is a small but robust museum. It's well worth the trip if you are interested in learning more about Indigenous peoples, especially the Lenape who lived in Pennsylvania. The Lenape were the native peoples who met with William Penn when he came to North America, and the museum presents a more complete telling of these early interactions. There are great artifacts throughout the museum, with options for self-guided or guided tours. They have an annual event in August—the Roasting Ears of Corn Festival—that features demos of heritage skills like weaving and starting a fire. The museum is next to the Little Lehigh Parkway, a gorgeous green space, where you can follow the Lenape Trail, a self-guided informational walk.

## 14 MUSEUM OF THE AMERICAN REVOLUTION

**101 South Third Street**
**Philadelphia, PA 19106; 215-253-6731**
**amrevmuseum.org**
***Fully accessible. Certified Autism center.***

The Museum of the American Revolution opened in 2017 and is a newer addition to the historic Old City neighborhood. The museum is modern and has many interactive and engaging elements. There's a definite family-friendly vibe here, and strollers are allowed throughout. A notable feature is Washington's Revolutionary War Tent, which is the real deal and only observable in the museum's theater during timed showings. The museum also offers many different kinds of tours, from walking tours of the historic neighborhood (Independence Hall and the Liberty Bell are close), to guided gallery tours. What I really enjoy about the museum is its focus on often-ignored stories from this time period, including those of African Americans, women, and Indigenous peoples.

## 15 NATIONAL CIVIL WAR MUSEUM

**One Lincoln Circle**
**Harrisburg, PA 17103; 717-260-1861**
**nationalcivilwarmuseum.org**
***Wheelchair accessible.***

If you've visited Gettysburg and still want to know more about the Civil War, the National Civil War Museum in Harrisburg takes a deeper dive into stories during and surrounding the war. The museum features interactive exhibits that examine the history leading up to the war, as well as photos, manuscripts, and artifacts centered on the people who lived and fought in this pivotal time in American history. The museum is located in Harrisburg's Reservoir Park, which is a public green space that has some stellar views.

## 16 NATIONAL CONSTITUTION CENTER

**525 Arch Street**
**Philadelphia, PA 19106; 215-409-6600**
**constitutioncenter.org**
***Fully accessible, with regular sensory-friendly days.***

The National Constitution Center is the only museum in the country dedicated entirely to the U.S. Constitution. It's a modern museum with fantastic interactive exhibits that tell the stories of the document's creation and eventual amendments. There's also an hourly live theatre performance called *Freedom Rising* that brings the historic document to life with a live narrator surrounded by a 360-degree multimedia presentation. Programs change daily, so there's almost always something new to experience. The museum features a rare copy of the Constitution from its first public printing in 1787. Don't miss Signer's Hall, where you can walk among life-size bronze statues of the founding fathers and snap a selfie or two with Alexander Hamilton or Ben Franklin. It's located close to Independence Hall (see pages 7–8).

## 17 PENNSYLVANIA MILITARY MUSEUM

51 Boal Avenue
Boalsburg, PA 16827; 814-466-6263
pamilmuseum.org
*Wheelchair accessible.*

If you come from a military family or just want to know more about the men and women from Pennsylvania who have served in the U.S. Armed Forces, the Pennsylvania Military Museum might make a great day trip for you. Located near Penn State University's main campus in the central part of the state, the museum tells the stories of military heroes and features military machinery both in the museum and on the grounds outside. They have 10,000 artifacts, "from teacups to tanks." If you don't want to pay, you can walk around the outside area, where you can see several tanks and battleship guns. Active duty military members and their families can visit for free.

## 18 THE PENNSYLVANIA STATE CAPITOL FREE

Commonwealth Avenue
Harrisburg, PA 17120; 800-868-7672
pacapitol.com
*Check map on website for wheelchair accessible entrances/buildings.*

If you live in Pennsylvania or just want to see the state government in action, a visit to the Pennsylvania Capitol Building is in order. There's a Welcome Center on-site and free, daily guided tours of the building that last about 30 minutes. You could also do a self-guided tour. If you'd like to sit in to watch state congress members debate laws or discuss policy during a legislative session, know that seating is first come, first served. There's some really lovely artwork throughout the Capitol Building, especially in the Rotunda. Be sure to look down to admire the Moravian tiles that make up the floor. The State Museum of Pennsylvania (see page 100) is close by, so consider combining the two spots for a great day trip.

## 19 VALLEY FORGE NATIONAL HISTORIC PARK FREE

1400 North Outer Line Drive
King of Prussia, PA 19406
610-783-1000
nps.gov/vafo
*Visitor center and some exhibits are wheelchair accessible.*

After a stunning defeat at the Battle of Germantown during the Revolutionary War, George Washington and his troops headed to Valley Forge, where they camped for the winter. This national historic park is great for both history buffs and outdoors enthusiasts alike. The park stretches 3,500 acres across woodlands and meadows where visitors can hike, bike, or walk. There's also a 10-mile driving tour where you can see all of the historic spots. On the tour you can see Washington's Headquarters, the lovely stone home where Washington once stayed. There's also Muhlenberg's Brigade that features nine reconstructed soldiers' huts that you can go inside. Start at the visitor center and plan to spend several hours on-site.

## 20 WEITZMAN NATIONAL MUSEUM OF AMERICAN JEWISH HISTORY

101 South Independence Mall East
Philadelphia, PA 19106; 215-923-3811
theweitzman.org
*Wheelchair accessible.*
*Assistive listening devices available.*
*Sensory backpacks available.*

Just steps away from Independence Hall is the Weitzman National Museum of American Jewish History, a Smithsonian affiliate. Through its exhibits and programming, the museum shares the history and contributions of Jews in America from the 1600s to today. The museum has more than 30,000 objects in its collection. The museum is family-friendly, with a number of installations geared toward children. The Weitzman also hosts regular "Family Days," offering hands-on programs like arts and crafts, living history, and storytelling. You'll know you've arrived when you see the giant yellow *YO/OY* sculpture out front, a popular photo spot.

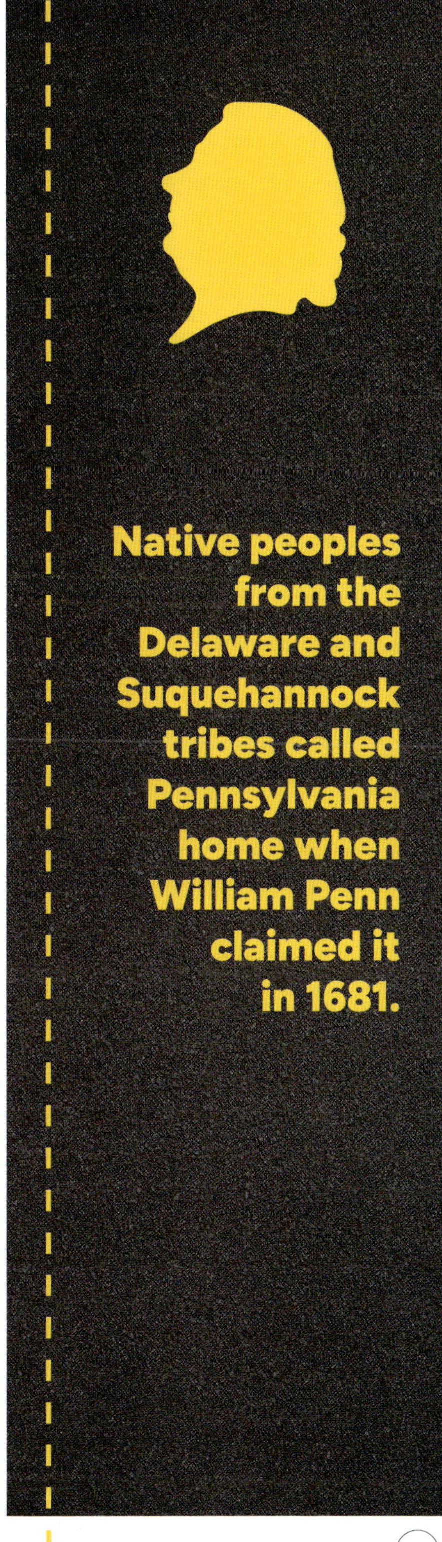

## Historic Philadelphia

The area surrounding Independence National Historical Park (see pages 7–8) has often been called "the most historic square mile" in America. There are so many historic spots in this tiny part of Philadelphia, it would be hard to visit them all in one day. The sites are peppered throughout the book, but there are too many to include with detailed descriptions. This list serves as a starting point for exploring this historic mile with some info about each place.

- Independence National Historical Park (see pages 7–8) is the centerpiece of the surrounding Old City neighborhood. In addition to the Liberty Bell Center, Independence Hall, and Congress Hall, there are numerous other buildings and sites to explore. A great place to start your visit is the Independence Visitor Center, which has a plethora of information and has staff that can help you make the most of your visit to this historic neighborhood.

- Ben Franklin founded the American Philosophical Society Museum, which is home to numerous rare books and manuscripts. Exhibits change annually.

- The President's House
When the National Park Service began planning to build a new home for the Liberty Bell in the early 2000s, an archeological exploration discovered remnants of George Washington's former home, including slave quarters. After much public controversy, the NPS created the exhibit *The President's House: Freedom and Slavery in the Making of a New Nation.* It is a 24-hour, open-air exhibit that traces the foundation of the home and tells the stories of those enslaved Africans who lived at the site.

- In 1744, Carpenters Hall hosted the First Continental Congress.

- Washington Square Park
A former burial ground that's now a popular park with benches. The Tomb of the Unknown Soldier of the American Revolution is located in the park.

- Mother Bethel A.M.E. Church The birthplace of the African Methodist Episcopal denomination. The historic church has numerous artifacts and is the final resting place for founder Reverend Richard Allen. Still holds weekly services.

• Arch Street Meeting House One of the original Quaker meeting houses in Philadelphia; it opened in 1682. Visitors can explore the grounds, museum space, and areas of worship. The Monthly Meeting of Friends of Philadelphia still worships here weekly and is welcoming of outside visitors interested in experiencing a Quaker meeting. The site is a National Historic Landmark.

• Benjamin Franklin Museum An underground museum dedicated to the life and works of Benjamin Franklin.

• Elfreth's Alley One of the country's oldest, continually inhabited streets featuring charming private homes and a historic cobblestone street.

• Christ Church and the Christ Church Burial Ground Historic church where the founding fathers worshipped. The gravesites of Ben Franklin and other signers of the Declaration of Independence are in the burial ground.

• Other sites in this book located in this historic neighborhood include: The Weitzman National Museum of American Jewish History (see page 11), Museum of the American Revolution (see page 9), National Liberty Museum (see page 35), Betsy Ross House (see pages 7–8), the African American Museum in Philadelphia (see page 5), the National Constitution Center (see pages 9–10), and Independence Seaport Museum (see page 8).

BRANDYWINE MUSEUM OF ART, CHADDS FORD

**Pennsylvania is the birthplace of fine art in America.**

The Pennsylvania Academy of the Fine Arts was the country's first art school and first fine arts museum. The state is also home to many more art museums, from smaller institutions to sprawling art meccas. The Philadelphia Art Museum is considered one of the finest in the world, its collection so vast that it's hard to see it all in one day. Some museums focus on a single artist or collection, while others span the history of art in both the Americas and across the globe. Whether you are an art aficionado or just someone who enjoys looking at engaging art, Pennsylvania has a day trip to suit your needs.

*Welcome to*

# ART MUSEUMS

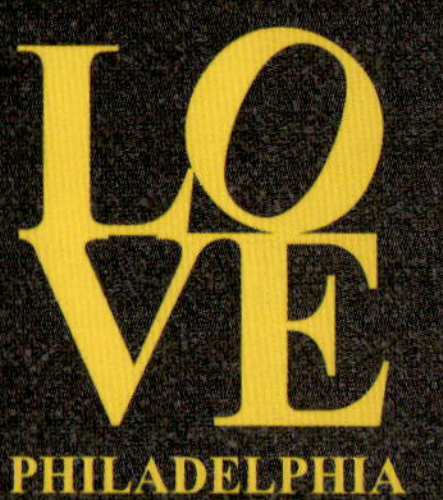


**In 1976, Robert Indiana's *LOVE* statue was nearly sold to a private buyer, but public outcry brought it back to Philly.**

*Find out more about*

# ART MUSEUMS

## 21 ALLENTOWN ART MUSEUM FREE

**31 North Fifth Street**
**Allentown, PA 18101; 610-432-4333**
**allentownartmuseum.org**
***Fully accessible.***

Walter Emerson Baum, a local artist, started the Allentown Art Museum during the 1930s. It had humble beginnings. At first, the museum consisted only of a small house, and it focused mostly on local artists. In the 1960s, businessman and art collector Samuel H. Kress donated 53 major works of art to the museum, pushing the museum to a new level. It has continued to grow and expand, with a robust permanent collection as well as regularly changing exhibits. It's a beautiful museum! Information about each piece is written in English and Spanish. Admission is free.

## 22 THE ANDY WARHOL MUSEUM

**117 Sandusky Street**
**Pittsburgh, PA 15212; 412-237-8300**
**warhol.org**
***Fully accessible.***

Pop Art icon Andy Warhol is a native son of Pittsburgh, and the city is home to The Andy Warhol Museum. While you can see a smattering of other artists' work, the focus here is on Warhol's life and art. The best way to explore the museum is to take the elevator up to the 7th floor and work your way down. You'll see the evolution of his artwork as you explore. There are paintings, sculptures, films, and videos to take in. Don't miss the *Silver Clouds* room where you can actually interact with the puffy, silver balloons. Insider tip: If you buy a membership to the Carnegie Museums, you'll get entrance to The Andy Warhol Museum, the Carnegie Museum of Natural History (see page 98), the Carnegie Museum of Art (see page 18), and the Carnegie Science Center (see page 98)—a fantastic deal if you are exploring the museums in Pittsburgh!

## 23 BARNES

**2025 Benjamin Franklin Parkway**
**Philadelphia, PA 19130; 215-278-7000**
**barnesfoundation.org**
***Fully accessible.***

Albert C. Barnes was an avid art collector on a mission to teach people how to better appreciate art. He collected numerous artworks from the Impressionist to the Modern era and displayed them in the original Barnes Foundation, located in the suburbs. In his will, Barnes stated that the stunning array of art should never be moved. But, after much controversy and legal wrangling, the collection was moved to Center City Philadelphia, where you can now see the esteemed collection, including works by Renoir, Cezanne, Picasso, Matisse, and Van Gogh, all still exhibited in Barnes' unique manner. The Barnes is just steps away from the Philadelphia Museum of Art (see page 20) if you'd like to have a full day of art immersion.

## 24 BRANDYWINE MUSEUM OF ART

**1 Hoffman's Mill Road**
**Chadds Ford, PA 19317; 610-388-2700**
**brandywine.org/museum**
***Wheelchair accessible. The studio spaces are partially accessible. See website for details.***

The Brandywine Museum of Art showcases the work of several members of the Wyeth family, Andrew, N.C., and Jamie, as well as other notable American artists. Visitors get an intimate look inside the artist studios of Andrew and N.C. Wyeth, in addition to visiting the museum's gallery space. Expect to see portraits, still lifes, and landscape paintings detailing the beautiful Brandywine Valley. Alongside its lovely permanent collection, the Brandywine Museum of Art also has changing exhibitions. The art museum's campus is surrounded by 5 acres of beauty with native plant gardens and a river trail. You can easily spend a day taking it all in.

## 25 CARNEGIE MUSEUM OF ART

**4400 Forbes Avenue**
**Pittsburgh, PA 15213; 412-622-3131**
**carnegieart.org**
***Wheelchair accessible, but limited access in a few galleries. Check map for details.***

The Carnegie Museum of Art shares space and admission with the Carnegie Museum of Natural History (see page 98). It's easy to get overwhelmed with all there is to see, but you can pack it all into a day and see both parts if you start early and have a plan. I'd do a bit of online research to make note of all of your "must-see" items and then map out where each is located. Consider spending the morning in one museum, grabbing lunch, and then visiting the other. The art collection is vast, and the building is gorgeous. Highlights include a stunning collection of modern and contemporary art featuring works by Pollock, Rothko, Hopper, and the Guerilla Girls, just to name a few.

## 26 THE DEMUTH MUSEUM FREE

**120 East King Street**
**Lancaster, PA 17602; 717-299-9940**
**demuth.org**
***Not accessible.***

The Demuth Museum is a charming homage to American artist Charles Demuth. Demuth's home, where he lived, painted, and even died, serves as a gallery space. Displayed throughout are rotating Demuth pieces, often featuring many of his beautiful watercolor paintings. He hobnobbed with the likes of Picasso and Duchamp and was a leader in the Precisionist movement in modern art. He traveled the world, but always came home to his birthplace and inspiration, Lancaster. As it's a smaller museum, plan to only spend about an hour here. And don't miss the lovely, brick-lined garden. Although admission is free, donations are encouraged.

## 27 ERIE ART MUSEUM

**20 East 5th Street**
**Erie, PA 16507; 814-459-5477**
**erieartmuseum.org**
***Wheelchair accessible.***

What started as The Art Club of Erie more than 100 years ago has morphed into a vibrant art museum. There's always something new to see, since the museum often changes visiting exhibitions. Check the website before your visit to find out what's on display. It's a great place to see regional and local artists, and there's a distinct focus on education. The museum also hosts special events and after-hours programs. The museum is very close to Presque Isle State Park (see pages 84–85), if you want to squeeze in some outside adventures.

## 28 INSTITUTE OF CONTEMPORARY ART UNIVERSITY OF PENNSYLVANIA FREE

**118 South 36th Street**
**Philadelphia, PA 19104; 215-898-5911**
**icaphila.org**
***Fully accessible.***

Contemporary art is the art of today. It's often experimental, which means it's always changing. The ICA in Philadelphia features changing exhibits showcasing artists who are not afraid to take risks. It's free to visit, and there are tours available if you want a guide to help you better understand the art. It's always a fun visit, and you'll likely see something unique you've never seen before.

## 29 JAMES A. MICHENER ART MUSEUM

**138 South Pine Street**
**Doylestown, PA 18901; 215-340-9800**
**michenerartmuseum.org**
***Fully accessible.***

The stately, stone walls are the first thing you'll see when you visit the James A. Michener Art Museum. It was once the Bucks County Prison, but now it's home to a lovely collection of American Art. Named after Doylestown native and novelist James A. Michener, the museum has an outdoor sculpture garden perfect for strolling. The art collection spans from American Impressionism to Modern and Contemporary. Plan to spend a few hours to see everything. Don't miss the Nakashima Reading Room, a tranquil space with beautiful furniture you can actually sit in. It's so cozy, you might want to stay awhile.

## 30 LANCASTER MUSEUM OF ART FREE

**135 North Lime Street**
**Lancaster, PA 17602; 717-394-3497**
**demuth.org/exhibitions-lma**
***First floor is wheelchair accessible.***

In 2014, the Lancaster Museum of Art and The Demuth Museum (see previous page) merged but remained separate and distinct museums. The Demuth focuses on Charles Demuth's home and lifework. The Lancaster Museum of Art focuses more on featuring the art of local artists and visiting exhibitions. They are only a few blocks from each other and worth a visit if you are an art lover. Check the website before visiting the Lancaster Museum of Art for two reasons. First, you'll know what is currently on exhibit, and second, to make sure it's open—it closes in between exhibits. Additionally, the website shows many of the museum's works of art even if they are not currently on display. Although admission is free, donations are encouraged.

## 31 MATTRESS FACTORY

**500 Sampsonia Way**
**Pittsburgh, PA 15212; 412-231-3169**
**mattress.org**
***Partial accessibility. Galleries at 500 Sampsonia are wheelchair accessible. Only the first floor of the other two buildings, 516 Sampsonia Way and 1414 Monterey Street, are wheelchair accessible.***

Mattress Factory is a contemporary art museum that is housed across three separate buildings. Start your visit at 500 Sampsonia Way, and then wind your way through the neighborhood to the other locations: 516 Sampsonia Way and 1414 Monterey Street. The exhibits at all three galleries are quirky and thought-provoking. Mattress Factory focuses its collection on installation art, so the exhibits are large and sometimes visually overwhelming. Expect to spend at least 2-3 hours exploring all three buildings.

## 32 PALMER MUSEUM OF ART FREE

**The Pennsylvania State University**
**650 Bigler Road**
**University Park, PA 16802;**
**814-865-7673**
**palmermuseum.psu.edu**
***Wheelchair accessible.***

The Palmer Museum of Art reopened in its newly built home in the summer of 2024. Housed on the Penn State campus, the museum sits next to the university's gorgeous gardens and arboretum (see page 52), so you can make it a whole day trip. The collection features paintings, sculptures, studio crafts, and decorative arts from around the world. It's the biggest art museum in Central Pennsylvania. The Palmer's permanent collection has items from across the globe and spans centuries, with paintings, sculptures, studio glass, ceramics, and works on paper. Admission is free, but donations are suggested.

## 33 PENNSYLVANIA ACADEMY OF THE FINE ARTS

**118-128 North Broad Street**
**Philadelphia, PA 19102; 215-972-7600**
**pafa.org**
***Wheelchair accessible.***

The Pennsylvania Academy of the Fine Arts was the first art school and art museum in the United States. Located in the heart of Center City Philadelphia, it houses thousands of works of American art from the 18th century to contemporary art. Plan to see works by the masters, including West, Eakins, Homer, Cassatt, Demuth, and Warhol, to name a few. You'll know you're in the right spot when you see the iconic 51-foot-tall Claes Oldenburg sculpture, *Paint Torch.* The Historic Landmark Building is itself a work of art, built by Frank Furness and George Hewitt.

## 34 PHILADELPHIA MUSEUM OF ART

**2600 Benjamin Franklin Parkway**
**Philadelphia, PA 19130; 215-763-8100**
**philamuseum.org**
***Fully accessible.***

One of the country's oldest art museums, the Philadelphia Museum of Art is one of my absolute favorite places to visit in Philadelphia. If you've seen the movie *Rocky* (see page 36), you'll immediately recognize the steps and stunning façade. The PMA has more than 200,000 objects and hosts exhibitions regularly. It's nearly impossible to see the entire museum in one day. My advice is to check out the museum's website and make a list of the sections and/or works of art that are must-see for you. I will never tire of seeing Van Gogh's *Sunflowers,* Picasso's *Three Musicians,* or any of Marcel Duchamp's works. I highly recommend visiting the *Ceremonial Teahouse* in the Asian Arts section and the *Fountain from the Monastery of Saint-Michel-de-cuxa.*

RODIN MUSEUM, PHILADELPHIA

## 35 RODIN MUSEUM

**2151 Benjamin Franklin Parkway**
**Philadelphia, PA 19130; 215-763-8100**
**rodinmuseum.org**
***Wheelchair accessible.***

Auguste Rodin is probably best known for *The Thinker* sculptures. You can see one of Rodin's versions of the iconic sculpture just by walking past the Rodin Museum. Managed by the nearby Philadelphia Museum of Art, the Rodin Museum is located on Benjamin Franklin Parkway and contains the largest collection of Rodin's works outside of Paris. Don't miss his looming *Gates of Hell* inspired by Dante's *Inferno.* It is a sight to behold. Admission is pay-what-you-wish. The museum is close to the Barnes (see page 17), the Academy of Natural Sciences (see page 98), and the Franklin Institute (see page 99).

## 36 WOODMERE ART MUSEUM

**9201 Germantown Avenue**
**Philadelphia, PA 19118; 215-247-0476**
**woodmereartmuseum.org**
***Mostly accessibility. All galleries but the balcony area are accessible.***

The Woodmere Art Museum is a smaller museum located in the Chestnut Hill neighborhood. Its focus is solely on Philadelphia artists. While there is a permanent collection, one of the best things about the Woodmere is that its exhibitions change often, so there's almost always something new to see. Don't miss all of the amazing sculptures located throughout the outdoor grounds. There's also a children's gallery with art from Philadelphia students. Woodmere also has great programming, including evening jazz and family-friendly events.

FEEDING GIRAFFES AT THE PHILADELPHIA ZOO, PHILADELPHIA

## Pennsylvania is a great state for bird-watchers and animal lovers.

Due to its geographic location, the state is often a stop for migrating birds to rest and refuel. Some of the spots in this chapter are outdoor spaces where you can grab your binoculars and connect to the natural world. This chapter also features some zoos where you can view exotic wildlife up close. I'm an extreme animal lover and consider them my kin. I know some people see zoos as controversial, but I believe that the ones on this list are doing research and conservation for the greater good.

*Welcome to*

# BIRD-WATCHERS & ANIMAL LOVERS

## *Find out more about* BIRD-WATCHERS & ANIMAL LOVERS

### 37 THE DISCOVERY CENTER FREE

3401 Reservoir Drive
Philadelphia, PA 19121; 610-990-3431
discoveryphila.org

***Mostly accessible. Visitor center is ADA-accessible, but trails may have some uneven surfaces.***

A formerly abandoned reservoir has become the focal point for The Discovery Center in Philadelphia's vast Fairmount Park system. The center is located in East Park and is right across the street from Smith Memorial Playground (see page 45). This family-friendly center is focused on education and encouraging families to get outside to enjoy the benefits of nature. Visitors can borrow binoculars from the visitor center and try to spy migrating birds refueling at the reservoir. The center is open 6 days a week and is always free. It's easily accessible via public transit. The Philadelphia Outward Bound School is also based at the center and offers public programming.

### 38 ELK COUNTRY VISITOR CENTER FREE

950 Winslow Hill Road
Benezette, PA 15821; 814-787-5167
elkcountryvisitorcenter.com

***Wheelchair-accessible visitor center, 4-D theater, trails, and viewing areas.***

Pennsylvania is home to the largest wild elk herd in the northeast. The Elk Country Visitor Center is the place to go to see elk in their native habitat. The center has exhibits where you can learn about the history and conservation of these majestic animals. The building has huge windows and scopes to help you spot elk across the panoramic view. There's also a theater and a special space for children to explore. There are three trails with viewing areas that are all wheelchair- and stroller-friendly. It's important to remember that elk are wild animals that don't adhere to schedules, but the best time to see them is in spring and summer months, early in the morning or near dusk.

### 39 ELMWOOD PARK ZOO

1661 Harding Boulevard
Norristown, PA 19401; 800-652-4143
elmwoodparkzoo.org

***Wheelchair accessible, though some terrain is steep. See zoo's accessibility map for guidance. Certified Autism Center with sensory backpacks available to borrow. Zoo also provides a sensory guide to the entire space.***

Elmwood Park Zoo is a smaller zoo located in the Philadelphia suburb of Norristown. The zoo's goal is to provide experiences that will encourage visitors to care more for wildlife and take action toward conservation. Elmwood Park Zoo has about 100 different species of animals, including giraffes, alligators, eagles, red pandas, otters, and many more. For an extra fee, visitors can book intimate experiences with the animals called "Elmwood Encounters." These activities include feeding the giraffes or otters or getting an up-close view of Penny the alligator as she plays with her toys. The zoo also hosts regular educational programming and has designated days when guests can bring their dogs.

## 40 HAWK MOUNTAIN SANCTUARY

**1700 Hawk Mountain Road**
**Kempton, PA 19529; 610-756-6961**
**hawkmountain.org**
***Wheelchair accessible trail and lookout, amphitheater, and visitor center.***

Hawk Mountain Sanctuary is a special place whether you are a bird nerd or not. The 2,600-acre green space along the Kittatinny Ridge is one of the best places in the state to see migrating hawks. There are hiking trails and viewing areas. I'm a big fan of packing a lunch and hiking the ridge to watch birds soaring above while having a picnic. The best time to see lots of hawks is in September and October, but the area is gorgeous, and the views are stunning year-round. The website has a seasonal description of what you can expect to see. Hawk Mountain is also super accessible for those with mobility challenges, with an ADA-accessible trail and viewing area.

## 41 MIDDLE CREEK WILDLIFE MANAGEMENT AREA FREE

**100 Museum Road**
**Stevens, PA 17578; 717-733-1512**
**advkeen.co/middlecreek**
***Wheelchair accessible.***

The Middle Creek Wildlife Management Area is 6,000 acres of protected green space in Central Pennsylvania. The biggest draw here is the annual arrival of thousands of snow geese. Nearly 100,000 stop by in the late winter each year and are a sight and sound to behold. There are also significant numbers of Canada Geese and Tundra Swans that stopover too. The best time to go is late February through early March, but there are updates and live streaming on the website. Expect crowds because the snow geese are popular. Dress warmly and bring a camera. Sunrise and sunset are your best chances to see large numbers. There's also a self-guided driving tour and 20 miles of hiking trails.

## 42 NATIONAL AVIARY

**700 Arch Street**
**Pittsburgh, PA 15212; 412-323-7235**
**aviary.org**
***Fully accessible. Sensory bags available. See website for accessibility map and info.***

If you are a bird nerd or are interested in getting some up-close views of hundreds of birds, add the National Aviary in Pittsburgh to your must-see list. This zoo is unique because it's dedicated solely to birds (and an occasional sloth). There are more than 500 birds on-site representing about 150 different species. The cool thing about the National Aviary is how it is set up: Each habitat is an open space with birds freely flying about. Warning: You may get pooped on. For an additional fee, visitors can feed some of the birds such as the penguins. My favorite spot is the wetlands habitat. So many flamingos!

## 43 PEACE VALLEY NATURE CENTER FREE

**170 North Chapman Road**
**Doylestown, PA 18901; 215-348-6270**
**peacevalleynaturecenter.org**
***Some trails are accessible.***

Peace Valley Nature Center is a beautifully tranquil spot situated along Lake Galena in Bucks County. I love visiting here and bird-watching at the bird blinds. A bird blind is kind of like a woodland closet where you can observe birds up close, but they can't see you. Stop by the Nature Center and grab a checklist to see how many different species of birds you can spot on your visit. If you don't have your own binoculars or are new to bird-watching, fret not! You can borrow a backpack with a field guide and binoculars during your visit. There are also 15 miles of hiking trails along wetland, meadow, and forest habitats. The center is close to Peace Valley Lavender Farm (see page 106) and Doylestown shopping (see page 111) and museums.

## 44 PHILADELPHIA ZOO

**3400 West Girard Avenue**
**Philadelphia, PA 19104; 215-243-1100**
**philadelphiazoo.org**
***Wheelchair accessible. Quiet areas map available.***

The Philadelphia Zoo was America's first Zoo, opened in 1874. It spans 42 acres and is brimming with animals. A unique thing about the Philadelphia Zoo is its Zoo360, which is a network of overhead see-through mesh wire trails where animals can roam. So, you might be walking along and spot a tiger or gorilla strolling above you. Personally, I love the giant river otters and the free-flight bird habitat, and I am a big fan of the reptile house. For a small fee, you can tack on extras to your zoo visit such as feeding a bird or giraffe or riding a carousel. Plan to spend an entire day here and wear good walking shoes.

## 45 PITTSBURGH ZOO & AQUARIUM

**7370 Baker Street**
**Pittsburgh, PA 15206; 412-665-3640**
**pittsburghzoo.org**
***Fully accessible. Sensory map available.***

The Pittsburgh Zoo & Aquarium is one of only a few places in the country to have both a zoo and aquarium together in one place. There's a lot to see here, so I recommend doing a bit of research ahead of time if there are must-see animals on your list. For a small fee, you can get a ride-all-day pass to the tram, which can make navigating the 77-acre park easier. There are also a few "wild encounters" for an extra fee where you can get up-close with some of the zoo's animals. There are more than 8,000 animals here, representing about 600 different species. Prepare to spend an entire day here to take in everything.

## 46 POWDERMILL NATURE RESERVE FREE

**1795 Route 381**
**Rector, PA 15677; 724-593-6105**
**carnegiemnh.org/visit-powdermill**
***Wheelchair accessible.***

About an hour and a half drive southeast of Pittsburgh is a lovely respite from city life. The Powdermill Nature Reserve is affiliated with the Carnegie Museum of Natural History (see page 98). It's a whopping 2,200 acres of outdoor space to explore for free. There's a nature center with exhibits about local flora, fauna, and ecosystems. It's a great spot for a family nature hike. The reserve is also a research center where scientists study local wildlife and is a great destination for group field trips. There are a variety of habitats to explore, including forests, ponds, meadows, and streams.

## 47 SHAVER'S CREEK ENVIRONMENTAL CENTER FREE

**3400 Discovery Road**
**Petersburg, PA 16669; 814-863-2000**
**shaverscreek.org**
***Wheelchair accessible.***

Shaver's Creek Environmental Center is a place of outdoor wonder. It's a great location to spend the day hiking and exploring the 7,000 acres of woodlands and marshes. The family-friendly center's focus is on education. In addition to hiking trails and a picnic area, there's also an aviary where you can visit resident hawks, owls, falcons, and eagles. Inside the nature center is a Discovery Room with exhibits that encourage kids to touch and feel natural objects. Visitors can also meet resident animals inside, including snakes, turtles, frogs, and the state amphibian, the Eastern Hellbender. Affiliated with Penn State, Shaver's Creek is in the central part of the state. Don't miss the fantastic book and gift shop!

## 48 WOLF SANCTUARY OF PENNSYLVANIA

**465 Speedwell Forge Road**
**Lititz, PA 17543; 717-626-4617**
**wolfsanctuarypa.org**
***Somewhat accessible. Terrain is relatively flat, but not paved. There are grass and rocks on the .25 mile tour. Contact to discuss accessibility needs.***

Wolves are often very misunderstood creatures. If you'd like to learn more about them and see some up close, head to the Wolf Sanctuary of Pennsylvania where about 50 gray wolves and wolf-dogs can live in a safe, natural environment. You can only visit by booking a tour ahead of time. The wolves are popular, so you'll probably need to buy tickets well in advance of your visit. The tours are held even in the rain and snow because wolves are wild animals who don't mind getting wet. Wear good walking shoes, as you'll walk about a quarter of a mile during the tour. If you are lucky, maybe you will get to howl along with some wolves.

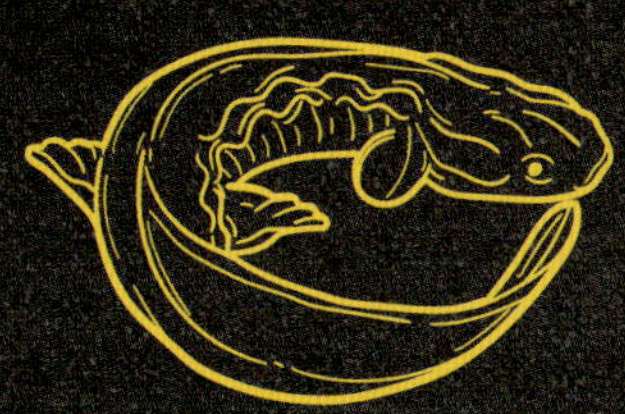

**The state amphibian, the eastern hellbender (also nicknamed "snot otter"), is a shy creature that likes to live under giant rocks in rivers and creeks, so chances are you won't see one easily.**

SENATOR JOHN HEINZ HISTORY CENTER, PITTSBURGH

## Pennsylvania is rich in cultural heritage.

The places in this chapter help us better understand and connect with our culture and shared humanity. Cultural heritage encompasses so many things, from artifacts and art to traditions, customs, and ways of living and speaking. Given the size and history of Pennsylvania, the cultural heritage represented here is diverse, which is something I love about the state. It truly is a melting pot. The list of places kept growing and growing until I forced myself to stop because cultural heritage is everywhere. I hope you will find these places as fun and fascinating to visit as I do.

Welcome to

# CULTURAL HERITAGE

NATIONAL LIBERTY MUSEUM, PHILADELPHIA

## Find out more about CULTURAL HERITAGE

### 49 AMERICAN TREASURE TOUR MUSEUM

One American Treasure Way
Oaks, PA 19456; 866-970-8687
americantreasuretour.com
*Wheelchair accessible.*

Think of the American Treasure Tour Museum as a fun-house, pop-culture version of the Mercer Museum (see page 34). You'll take a narrated tram car through its wildly eclectic collection of oversize signs, statues, toys, antique cars, movie memorabilia, and animatronics, giving amusement-park vibes to what is essentially a massive warehouse of randomly arranged artifacts from the last century or so. The delights/horrors include a 20-foot Gumby, a thousand Raggedy Anns, countless calliopes, Mummers gear, uranium glass, a replica of the Ark of the Covenant, and a terrifying assemblage of screaming baby dolls. It's nostalgic, it's creepy, it's surprisingly not dusty, and it's got endless selfie opportunities. The museum is also close to Valley Forge National Historic Park (see pages 10–11).

### 50 THE AMISH VILLAGE

199 Hartman Bridge Road
Ronks, PA 17572; 717-687-8511
amishvillage.com
*Contact site for accessibility information.*

Pennsylvania has one of the largest Amish communities in the country, and visitors to Lancaster and Pennsylvania Dutch Country love to seek out its culture to get a closer look. The Amish settled in the state in the 1700s and continue to live today much as they did back then. You will still see them traveling by foot or horse and buggy. The Amish Village is a commercial site that educates visitors about Amish culture. Tours are offered through a 12-acre Amish farm and village, as well as guided bus tours through the vast farmlands of the Lancaster area.

### 51 THE AUGUST WILSON AFRICAN AMERICAN CULTURAL CENTER FREE

980 Liberty Avenue
Pittsburgh, PA 15222; 412-339-1011
awaacc.org
*Wheelchair accessible.*
*Assistive listening devices available.*
*ASL and live audio description available at certain events.*

The August Wilson African American Cultural Center is located in downtown Pittsburgh, in the heart of the city's cultural district. This cultural center celebrates Black arts and culture and is named after Pittsburgh native son and award-winning playwright August Wilson. On a visit to the center, you might experience music like a jazz or blues festival, literature like poetry, or theatrical performances. The center also has exhibit space showcasing art from African American artists. A permanent exhibit, *August Wilson: The Writer's Landscape*, tells the story of Wilson, a recipient of numerous Tony Awards and Pulitzer Prizes.

## 52 ECKLEY MINERS' VILLAGE MUSEUM

**2 Eckley Back Road**
**Weatherly, PA 18255; 570-636-2070**
**eckleyminersvillage.com**
***Partially accessible. Not all buildings are wheelchair accessible.***

Northeastern Pennsylvania became home to generations of immigrants who settled in the area to work in the anthracite coal mines. Eckley Miners' Village is a historic company coal town, where miners once lived with their families. You can tour the 19th-century town to see what life was like back then. The mile-long stretch features about 50 homes and 100 outbuildings, and visitors can go inside several buildings, such as the church. There are guided tours and occasional living-history events. Wear comfortable walking shoes and plan to spend about two to three hours on-site if you want to see everything. The historic site is near Hickory Run State Park (see pages 129–130).

## 53 EDGAR ALLAN POE NATIONAL HISTORIC SITE FREE

**532 North 7th Street**
**Philadelphia, PA 19123; 215-965-2305**
**nps.gov/edal**
***Museum area is wheelchair accessible, but the historic home is not.***

Edgar Allan Poe is one of my favorite authors, so I love that I can visit his Philadelphia home whenever I want some creepy inspiration. The Edgar Allan Poe National Historic Site is the house where Poe lived and wrote many of his epic tales of horror and suspense. And the place is sufficiently eerie to walk through. There's a lovely exhibit on the first floor about Poe's life and works. The house is sparsely furnished, but you can explore all levels, including the very dimly lit cellar, no doubt the inspiration for his hair-raising tales. His six years living in this space are believed to be his most prolific.

## 54 FALLINGWATER

**1491 Mill Run Road**
**Mill Run, PA 15464; 724-329-8501**
**fallingwater.org**
***Some wheelchair accessibility. Assisted Listening Devices available. Check website for detailed accessibility information.***

Fallingwater is the iconic house Frank Lloyd Wright designed to blend organically with nature. Cantilevers support the house over the waterfall, which is the namesake of the property. You can tour both the house and grounds, but the site is incredibly popular. Plan to reserve tickets for a guided tour at least 4-6 weeks ahead of a visit during peak times in July, August, and October. There are a variety of themed tours, including preservation, architecture, in-depth, and private. You can also purchase a ticket to just walk the grounds, which are vast and gorgeous. The surrounding Bear Run Nature Reserve is a mature hemlock forest with miles of trails. The towering rhododendron bushes throughout bloom from late June through mid-July and are simply stunning.

POE EXHIBIT, PHILADELPHIA

## 55 THE FRICK PITTSBURGH MUSEUM & GARDENS FREE

**7227 Reynolds Street**
**Pittsburgh, PA 15208; 412-371-0600**
**thefrickpittsburgh.org**
***Many buildings are wheelchair accessible. Website has detailed accessibility information.***

The Frick Pittsburgh Museum & Gardens is a unique place with a wide variety of experiences. Here visitors can tour the sprawling mansion where industrialist Henry Clay Frick lived with his family during the Gilded Age. There's also an art museum with numerous pieces of furniture, decorative pieces, and paintings. The Car & Carriage Museum is another building on the campus that displays historic carriages and early automobiles. There are 10 acres of beautifully landscaped gardens and a gorgeous greenhouse. Grab a bite to eat at the café on-site or sip tea while enjoying the surroundings. You can easily spend the better part of a day exploring this place.

## 56 HISTORIC EPHRATA CLOISTER

**632 West Main Street**
**Ephrata PA 17522; 717-733-6600**
**ephratacloister.org**
***Much of site is wheelchair accessible. Historic buildings have narrow doorways, so visitors may borrow a wheelchair on-site that will fit. Contact ahead of time to discuss accessibility needs.***

The Historic Ephrata Cloister was once the site of a monastic community. Conrad Beissel, who wished to live the life of a hermit as he waited for the end of the world, founded the site in 1732. Eighty celibate community members joined him. They wore white robes and dedicated their lives to serving God. They farmed, made paper, built things, and lived a very simple life. You can tour the 30-acre site and get an up-close look at nine historic buildings. There are guided tours, but much of the site is self-guided. It's located in Pennsylvania Dutch Country and would take up only part of a day trip to the area. Expect to spend about two hours exploring the site.

## 57 JOHN F. KENNEDY PLAZA (LOVE PARK) FREE

**1569 John F. Kennedy Boulevard**
**Philadelphia, PA 19102; 215-344-8544**
**phlvisitorcenter.com/lovepark**
***Public park with wheelchair accessibility.***

It seems that everyone who comes to Philadelphia takes two iconic photos: one in LOVE Park and the other in front of the Rocky statue (see page 36). John F. Kennedy Plaza is the official name of the public square, right across the street from Philadelphia's City Hall. But everyone in Philly calls it LOVE Park, named after Robert Indiana's famous *LOVE* statue. There are usually food trucks nearby, and there's an official visitor center on-site. LOVE Park is close to so many attractions, including the Franklin Institute (see page 99), the Academy of Natural Sciences (see page 98), the Barnes (see page 17), and the Philadelphia Museum of Art (see page 20). And if you stop by on a Wednesday in the warmer months, you might just see a wedding.

## 58 LANDIS VALLEY VILLAGE & FARM MUSEUM

**2451 Kissel Hill Road**
**Lancaster, PA 17601; 717-569-0401**
**landisvalleymuseum.org**
***Many buildings are wheelchair accessible. Access information available on website.***

Pennsylvania Germans, also known as Pennsylvania Dutch, began migrating to Pennsylvania in the late 1600s, seeking religious freedom. This community included Amish, Mennonite, Moravian, and others. The Landis Valley Village & Farm Museum honors the culture and heritage of this group from the 1700s to the mid-20th century. The living history museum has numerous buildings to explore, with one of the largest collections of PA German artifacts in the country. Plan to see demonstrations and authentic household items and tools. Budget at least three hours to see everything at the family-friendly site. Landis Valley is also home to the Heirloom Seed Project, which saves and sells seeds that were vital to PA Germans, including flax.

## 59 LAUREL HILL EAST & WEST FREE

### 59A Laurel Hill East

**3822 Ridge Avenue**
**Philadelphia, PA 19132; 610-668-9900**

### 59B Laurel Hill West

**225 Belmont Avenue**
**Bala Cynwyd, PA 19004; 610-668-9900**
**laurelhillphl.com**

***Both sites have many paved trails that are wheelchair accessible, but know that both sites have areas with steep inclines.***

Laurel Hill East & West are cemeteries that double as arboretums. They are united on paper but discontinuous in land. Laurel Hill East is located in Philadelphia overlooking the Schuylkill River, while Laurel Hill West is in the nearby suburb of Bala Cynwyd. Together they represent stunning examples of the rural cemetery movement, with Laurel Hill East being the second garden cemetery in the country. East opened in 1836 and, when space became an issue, West opened in 1869. These hallowed grounds were essentially public parks before such a thing existed. The Arboretum at Laurel Hill encompasses both sites and has more than 6,500 trees and shrubs. Both sites are the final resting places for numerous famous Philadelphians and feature beautiful monuments, headstones, and mausoleums.

## 60 MERCER MUSEUM & FONTHILL CASTLE

**84 South Pine Street**
**Doylestown, PA 18901; 215-345-0210**
**East Court Street & Route 313**
**Doylestown, PA 18901; 215-348-9461**
**mercermuseum.org**

***Mercer Museum has partial wheelchair accessibility on the upper floors. The ground floor containing changing exhibits is completely accessible. Limited accessibility at Fonthill Castle. Contact prior to visit to discuss accessibility needs.***
***Note: There's no air-conditioning in most of the museum, so hot, humid days might be sweaty or challenging for those with health conditions.***

Henry Mercer was a Renaissance man. When he saw the Industrial Revolution unfolding, he decided to begin collecting items of daily use. He opened a museum with more than 30,000 artifacts to capture how Americans lived before industrialization. The museum can be visually overwhelming, but that is part of its charm. You'll easily spend a few hours lingering and learning about historic tools and trade. The museum has a lovely modern space on the first floor that's fully climate-controlled and houses changing exhibits. Fonthill Castle was Mercer's home and display area for his famed Moravian tiles. It's about a mile away and has a separate entrance fee. The concrete castle has 44 rooms and 200+ windows.

MERCER MUSEUM, DOYLESTOWN

## 61 NATIONAL LIBERTY MUSEUM

**321 Chestnut Street**
**Philadelphia, PA, 19106**
**215-925-2800**
**libertymuseum.org**
***Wheelchair accessible.***

Nestled in Philadelphia's historic district, just steps away from Independence Hall (see pages 7–8), is a museum dedicated entirely to the concept of liberty. The National Liberty Museum is part art museum and part history museum with a mission to engage visitors around the ideas of liberty and freedom. The museum changes exhibits often but also has permanent ones. Its *Heroes from Around the World* exhibit tells the stories of people who embraced liberty, such as Gandhi and Mother Teresa. The centerpiece of the museum is a fire-red, glass Dale Chihuly sculpture entitled *Flame of Liberty* that is breathtaking.

## 62 PENN MUSEUM

**3260 South Street**
**Philadelphia, PA 19104; 215-898-4000**
**penn.museum**
***Wheelchair accessible.***

The Penn Museum is connected to the University of Pennsylvania in Philadelphia. The museum used to be named the Museum of Archaeology and Anthropology, so it is brimming with fascinating artifacts from across the world arranged geographically. One of the museum's most remarkable artifacts is a 13-ton granite sphinx from Ancient Egypt. In fact, the Penn Museum has one of the largest collections in the country of Egyptian and Nubian items. The museum is huge, so plan to spend ample time exploring. There are gardens outside with fountains and ponds, a perfect spot to grab a snack or lunch on a sunny day. The museum hosts a full calendar of events, including after-hours family-friendly programming.

## 63 PHILADELPHIA'S MAGIC GARDENS

**1020 South Street**
**Philadelphia, PA 19147; 215-733-0390**
**phillymagicgardens.org**
***Limited wheelchair accessibility.***
***Sensory bags available.***
***Touch tours available for those with vision loss. Detailed accessibility information on website.***

Philadelphia's Magic Gardens is a space like no other. Mosaic artist and muralist Isaiah Zagar and his wife had lived in the South Street neighborhood in Philadelphia for decades when he began creating mosaic murals in vacant lots near his studio as a form of therapy. Using handmade tiles, mirrors, bottles, bicycle wheels, and a variety of other mixed media, the mosaics continued to grow. When the owner of the lots tried to sell and tear down the art, the community rallied to save it. Now, Philadelphia Magic Gardens is a destination where you can see Zagar's saved work up close. There are two indoor galleries and two levels of an outdoor sculpture garden.

## 64 ROCKY STATUE FREE

**2600 Benjamin Franklin Parkway**
**Philadelphia, PA 19130; 925-316-3642**
**rockystatue.com**
***Wheelchair accessible via sidewalk curb cutouts.***

Every time I drive by the Rocky Statue, there's a line of people waiting to take photos. The fictional Rocky Balboa became legend in the 1976 film *Rocky*. Played by Sylvester Stallone, Rocky gets the chance to fight the heavyweight champ of the world. Rocky trains hard, and his workout includes running up the many steps to the Philadelphia Museum of Art (see page 20) where he thrusts his hands in the air in victory. In 1980, Stallone commissioned artist A. Thomas Schomberg to make the statue for *Rocky III*. The work of art now lives at the foot of the steps, so you can get your photo taken with Rocky and then run up the steps while humming "Gonna Fly Now."

ROCKY STATUE, PHILADELPHIA

## 65 THE ROSENBACH

**2008-2010 Delancey Place**
**Philadelphia, PA 19103; 215-732-1600**
**rosenbach.org**
***Wheelchair accessible from rear entrance.***

If you consider yourself a book nerd, then get thee to The Rosenbach. Both a museum and library, The Rosenbach has an impressive collection of rare books and manuscripts. Dr. A.S.W. Rosenbach and his brother Philip were rare book dealers, so it's no surprise that the collection contains books spanning centuries. You can only explore the collection and historic house museum through a guided tour (and you can make an appointment with a librarian to view specific titles up close). Here are just a few names gracing the shelves: Cervantes, Chaucer, Shakespeare, Burns, Carroll, Stoker, Dickenson, Joyce, and Wheatly. The museum also has a reconstruction of Marianne Moore's Greenwich Village living room and nearly all of her manuscripts and correspondence.

## 66 SENATOR JOHN HEINZ HISTORY CENTER

**1212 Smallman Street**
**Pittsburgh, PA 15222; 412-454-6000**
**heinzhistorycenter.org**
***Fully accessible.***

The Senator John Heinz History Center is located in the heart of downtown Pittsburgh, not far from the convention center. This Smithsonian-affiliated museum centers its collections around the history and heritage of Western Pennsylvania. One of its special collections is the rebuilt set from *Mister Rogers' Neighborhood,* along with numerous artifacts from the beloved show. The history of the H.J. Heinz Co. is on display as well, including an 11-foot ketchup bottle made of smaller bottles. It is a sight to behold. I really love the museum's glass collection, showcasing 200 years of Pittsburgh glass. The Western Pennsylvania Sports Museum is located on the second and third floors of the museum.

## 67 SHOFUSO JAPANESE CULTURAL CENTER

**West Fairmount Park**
**Horticultural and Lansdowne Drives**
**Philadelphia, PA 19131; 215-878-5097**
**japanphilly.org/shofuso/**
***Building is not wheelchair accessible.***

Shofuso Japanese Cultural Center is a traditional Japanese house that was actually built in Japan. It was exhibited at the Museum of Modern Art before moving to Philadelphia. Shofuso is surrounded by a stunning display of cherry trees that bloom in April. Each year, Shofuso hosts a popular cherry blossom festival. I love walking through the cherry blossoms when a light breeze blows and creates a snowfall of flower petals. The center hosts events focused on Japanese culture, including tea ceremony demonstrations and Japanese language instruction. Artist Hiroshi Senju's beautiful murals inside create a tranquil backdrop. Outside, there's also a koi pond and Japanese gardens.

## 68 WHARTON ESHERICK MUSEUM

**1520 Horseshoe Trail**
**Malvern, PA 19355; 610-644-5822**
**whartonesherickmuseum.org**
***Partial wheelchair accessibility in studio. Contact museum ahead of time to discuss accessibility needs.***

Wharton Esherick was an artist, sculptor, and poet who is probably best known for his wood furniture creations. He's considered a leader in the studio furniture movement and his pieces are exhibited at museums up and down the East Coast. You can tour his home and studio to get an intimate look at the space where he lived and created. The museum hosts different themed tours, and you must make reservations ahead of time to visit. The site is tucked into 12 acres of woodlands and features several historic buildings. The museum is closed to visits and tours in January and February each year.

OUTDOOR NATURAL PLAYGROUND, NED SMITH CENTER FOR NATURE & ART, MILLERSBURG

## Don't forget to plan trips for the whole family!

While many of the destinations in this book are perfect for all ages, this chapter focuses on those special places where young ones get to play and be kids. In these spaces, children are encouraged to explore, touch things, and get messy. There are indoor places perfect for rainy days, as well as outdoor spots where kids can connect to nature in a safe and fun way. There are even a few amusement parks that are sure to delight even the adults in your group.

# Welcome to FAMILY FUN

**Crayola sold its first box of Crayons in 1903 for a nickel.**

CRAYOLA EXPERIENCE, EASTON

## *Find out more about* FAMILY FUN

### 69 BUCKS COUNTY CHILDREN'S MUSEUM

**500 Union Square Drive**
**New Hope, PA 18938; 215-693-1290**
**buckskids.org**
***Wheelchair accessible.***
***Sensory backpacks available.***

Engaging kids in constructive play is the focus at the Bucks County Children's Museum located in New Hope. The museum is popular, so you should buy tickets in advance of your visit. Here, kids can become doctors and nurses, design and build things, shop like a grownup at a grocery store, dig for fossils, move boats through water using an interactive lock system, and sail through the skies in a virtual hot-air balloon. The 10,000-square-foot space is sure to delight young visitors and keep them busy for hours.

### 70 CHILDREN'S MUSEUM OF PITTSBURGH

**10 Children's Way, Allegheny Square**
**Pittsburgh, PA 15212; 412-322-5058**
**pittsburghkids.org**
***Fully accessible. Sensory tools available. Check website for specific sensory-friendly afternoon scheduling.***

The Children's Museum of Pittsburgh is in a great location, close to numerous other sites like the National Aviary (see page 25) and the Carnegie Science Center (see page 98). This museum has something for all interests. I love its newest permanent exhibit—a kindness gallery channeling the spirit of Fred Rogers. There are also installations that get creative juices flowing, where children can design and create art. Several spaces encourage kids to tumble, climb, bounce, or spin. In warmer months, there's an outdoor garden and an opportunity to play in the mud. There's also a nursery for quiet time if the littles need a break.

### 71 CRAYOLA EXPERIENCE

**30 Centre Square**
**Easton, PA 18042; 610-515-8000**
**crayolaexperience.com/easton**
***Wheelchair accessible.***

The maker of everyone's favorite crayon—Crayola—has its corporate headquarters right here in Pennsylvania. The world was introduced to Crayola crayons in 1903, and for many years you could tour the factory in Easton. Now, families flock to the Crayola Experience, an indoor color playground. Imagine 65,000 square feet of all of your favorite Crayola products to play with, along with interactive exhibits that make the colors come to life. Visitors can name and wrap personalized crayons or create instant cartoons of themselves to color. At the Crayon Factory Show, families can learn about the magic and science behind the making of crayons. The Crayola Experience features more than 20 hands-on attractions that will keep you and your little ones creating for hours. Plan to spend about three to four hours exploring, and make sure you visit the store to load up on everything Crayola.

WATERPARK SECTION OF HERSHEY PARK, HERSHEY

## 72 EXPERIENCE CHILDREN'S MUSEUM

**420 French Street**
**Erie, PA 16507; 814-453-3743**
**eriechildrensmuseum.org**
***Wheelchair accessible.***
***Sensory backpacks available.***

The ExpERIEnce Children's Museum has a focus on STEAM-themed activities and exhibits. STEAM = Science, Technology, Engineering, Art, and Math. The exhibits are aimed to engage a large range of ages, from babies up to middle-school-aged children. There are exhibits about recycling and flight, as well as opportunities to construct and make art. The outdoor area is a certified Nature Explore classroom with space for water play, digging, building, making music, gardening, and reading. I love that there's a designated book nook for reading. Indoor exhibits engage kids in tinkering and building, and a special exhibit is focused on Lake Erie. This museum is close to Presque Isle State Park (see pages 84–85) and the Erie Maritime Museum (see page 6).

## 73 HERSHEY PARK

**100 West Hersheypark Drive**
**Hershey, PA 17033**
**717-534-3900**
**hersheypark.com**
***Wheelchair accessible.***
***Sensory backpacks available.***
***Check website for more information.***

Hershey Park is a destination sure to fill a full day with fun and memories. It's expansive, and admission includes three parks in one. Hershey Park is all about rides, including 15 roller coasters. There's also a water park called the Boardwalk, where you'll find water slides, cabanas, and a lazy river. ZooAmerica has animals from all over the North American continent, from common animals like bears and crocodiles to less common ones like ocelots or gila monsters. You'll also meet Hershey characters along the way. Hershey Park is also close to Hershey's Chocolate World (see page 74) and Hershey Gardens (see page 52), but I bet you'll run out of time at the park before you see everything.

## 74 KNOEBELS AMUSEMENT PARK FREE

391 Knoebels Boulevard, Route 487
Elysburg, PA 17824; 800-487-4386
knoebels.com
*Wheelchair accessible.*
*Low-sensory room.*

Knoebels Amusement Park in Elysburg is an old-fashioned amusement park with tons of rides, games, and food, kind of like a ginormous carnival. Admission is free to enter the park, but to ride any rides, you'll need to purchase tickets or an all-day pass. Rides include new and old-school wooden roller coasters, bumper cars, carousels, a Ferris wheel, and so much more. There are games galore where you can try to win some cool prizes. There's a lot to see and experience here, so prepare to be on the move all day.

## 75 LINVILLA ORCHARDS FREE

137 West Knowlton Road
Media, PA 19063; 610-876-7116
linvilla.com
*Wheelchair accessible but beware of uneven terrain.*

Linvilla Orchards is a lovely place that is always buzzing with activities. It's a popular place, likely because there's so much to do. I'm a big fan of the pick-your-own fields. You pick out a bag or box and pay ahead, then hop on a hayride to travel through the fields to harvest fresh fruit. But there's so much more at this farm! There are barnyard animals to meet, including goats, sheep, and horses. There's also a sizable playground, fishing in a stocked lake, and pumpkins galore in the fall. Linvilla also hosts a variety of festivals, so check the calendar on the website before your visit to see what's going on.

## 76 MT. AIRY ORCHARDS FREE

522 East Mount Airy Road
Dillsburg, PA 17019; 717-432-2544
mtairyorchards.com
*Farm store is wheelchair accessible.*

For some old-fashioned farm fun, head to Mt. Airy Orchards in Dillsburg. The working farm has a variety of pick-your-own fruit, including strawberries, blueberries, and blackberries, with apple and pumpkin picking in the autumn months. You can book a tractor-ride tour of the farm for a group. Don't miss the Playland area, where you'll find a lots of opportunities to jump, run, and slide. The straw bale mountain is especially fun to climb. If you go in the fall, be sure to check out the corn maze—a 5-acre site carved out for endless exploring.

## 77 NED SMITH CENTER FOR NATURE & ART FREE

176 Water Company Road
Millersburg, PA 17061; 717-692-3699
nedsmithcenter.org
*Building is wheelchair accessible. Inquire before visit about trail accessibility.*

The Ned Smith Center for Nature & Art is a huge outdoor space with a natural playground, trails, and a center with an art gallery. When you enter, you'll see Nature's Discovery Play Area, a playground completely constructed of natural wood objects. There are lots of well-marked trails to explore where you might happen upon wildlife. Pack a lunch to enjoy at one of the many picnic areas. The outdoor space is leashed-dog friendly, if you consider your pooch part of the family. Ned Smith was a Pennsylvania naturalist and artist, so the center combines a love of the outdoors with art. The indoor gallery space features Smith's work along with changing exhibits of local and national artists.

## 78 POCONO ENVIRONMENTAL EDUCATION CENTER

538 Emery Road
Dingmans Ferry, PA 18328
570-828-2319
peec.org
*Designated "Trail for Everyone," that is wheelchair accessible.*

The Pocono Environmental Education Center, commonly called "PEEC," is nestled within the Delaware Water Gap National Recreation Area (see pages 82–83). It's a space dedicated to educating and connecting youth to the natural world. It has a packed calendar of events and programming, so check the website ahead of your visit. There are also several hiking trails—all loops so nobody gets lost—to explore and enjoy. Grab a map before heading out; some are easy trails, while others are more rugged. There's a waterfall you can hike to on the 3-mile Tumbling Waters trail. I love the "Trail for Everyone," which is a wheelchair-accessible sensory trail.

## 79 PLEASE TOUCH MUSEUM

Memorial Hall
4231 Avenue of the Republic
Philadelphia, PA 19131; 215-581-3181
pleasetouchmuseum.org
*Wheelchair accessible. Quiet kits available. Scheduled limited-senses visiting hours.*

I have been to the Please Touch Museum numerous times and left every time with tuckered, happy children. Museums are usually places where kids must practice restraint, but not at Please Touch. Here, kids are meant to grab, feel, climb, and explore. Kids can become doctors or drivers, learn how to shop at a grocery store, and let their imaginations run wild. I love the Wonderland section, where you can join Alice and friends down the rabbit hole and even have make-believe tea with the Mad Hatter. If you have a child with sensory sensitivities, check the website for "Play Without Boundaries" hours, where the museum is closed to the public so the space is quieter.

MAD HORSE CAROUSEL AT PLEASE TOUCH MUSEUM, PHILADELPHIA

## 80 SESAME PLACE

**100 Sesame Road**
**Langhorne, PA 19047; 215-702-3566**
**sesameplace.com/philadelphia/**

***Fully accessible. See website for extensive accessibility information guide. Certified Autism Center.***

Who doesn't love *Sesame Street?* Sesame Place is a child's dream come true, where kids can meet and interact with their favorite *Sesame Street* characters. The amusement park is also full of rides that even kids-at-heart will enjoy. There are regular shows and parades. The park is huge—around 14 acres—so it's hard to pack it all into one day. Wear good walking shoes and plan to spend the entire day exploring. For families who have children with special needs, the website has an impressively detailed accessibility guide, so check that out before your visit. There are also low-sensory areas and sensory aids you can borrow.

## 81 SMITH MEMORIAL PLAYGROUND FREE

**3500 Reservoir Drive**
**Philadelphia, PA 19121; 215-765-4325**
**smithplayground.org**

***Partially accessible. Outdoors is wheelchair accessible, as is the first floor of the indoor play space.***

If you watch ABC's television show *Abbott Elementary*, you might have seen the episode where the school takes a field trip to Smith Memorial Playground. This free indoor and outdoor play space is historic and has been delighting families for more than 100 years. The huge wooden slide is famous and a favorite spot for children and adults alike. The outdoor area covers about 6 acres and has so many different pieces of playground equipment. There's also a certified Nature Explore Classroom for unstructured natural play. The indoor space has rotating "Play-stallations" along with an indoor playground and library. Smith Memorial Playground is right across the street from The Discovery Center (see page 24).

SMITH PLAYGROUND PHILADELPHIA

PUNXSUTAWNEY GROUNDHOG CLUB HANDLER A.J. DEREUME HOLDS PUNXSUTAWNEY PHIL AT THE ANNUAL GROUNDHOG DAY FESTIVITIES AT GOBBLER'S KNOB IN PUNXSUTAWNEY

**Festivals and annual events are a great way to pack a day with excitement.**

Pennsylvanians love festivals, bazaars, and any excuse to come together as a community to celebrate. The Bloomsburg Fair is a beloved annual tradition where you can always get your funnel cake needs met. And, each February, the country tunes in to see what Phil has to say about winter. I focused on the biggest events, but there is a seemingly endless number each year, so whatever your interest, I bet you can find a festival to celebrate it.

*Welcome to*

# FESTIVALS & ANNUAL EVENTS

**82** **BLOOMSBURG FAIR**

Bloomsburg, September
bloomsburgfair.com

**83** **GOSCHENHOPPEN FOLK FESTIVAL**

Perkiomenville, August
goschenhoppen.org

**84** **GROUNDHOG DAY FESTIVAL**

Punxsutawney, February
groundhog.org

**85** **LITTLE LEAGUE WORLD SERIES**

Williamsport, August
littleleague.org

**86** **MUSIKFEST**

Bethlehem, August
musikfest.org

**87** **PENNSYLVANIA FARM SHOW**

Harrisburg, January
farmshow.pa.gov

**88** **PENNSYLVANIA SHAKESPEARE FESTIVAL**

Center Valley, Spring—Summer
pashakespeare.org

**89** **PHILADELPHIA FOLK FESTIVAL**

Harleysville, August
folkfest.org

**90** **RENAISSANCE FAIRE**

Manheim, August—October
parenfaire.com/faire

The Philadelphia area has been dubbed "America's Garden Capital," featuring 30 gardens within 30 miles of the city (americasgardencapital.org). The Pennsylvania Horticultural Society's annual Philadelphia Flower Show attracts thousands of visitors from across the country. Gardens abound throughout Pennsylvania, making it likely that there is a garden nearby wherever your day trips might take you. Spring and summer are the best times to visit many of these gardens, but those with natural woodlands shine in the fall and winter months.

# *Welcome to* GARDENS, FLOWERS & ARBORETUMS

**The Pennsylvania state flower is the Mountain Laurel, the state tree is the Eastern Hemlock, the state bird is the ruffed grouse, and the state insect is the firefly.**

**103 TYLER ARBORETUM** ........... 55
**Media**
An arboretum with trails, a meadow maze, and natural woodlands.

A SEQUOIA TREE AT THE TYLER ARBORETUM, MEDIA

# *Find out more about*
# GARDENS, FLOWERS & ARBORETUMS

## 91 BARTRAM'S GARDENS FREE

**5400 Lindbergh Boulevard**
**Philadelphia, PA 19143; 215-729-5281**
**bartramsgarden.org**
***Some wheelchair accessibility. See website for details.***

Bartram's Gardens is a special place. The National Historic Landmark spans 50 acres, located on the Schuylkill River in an otherwise industrial area. The site features the 1700s home of botanist John Bartram along with other historic stone buildings. The gardens claim the title of the oldest surviving botanic garden in North America. The focus here is on native plants the Bartram family collected, as indicated through historic documents. The woodland area is particularly stunning in the fall. There are numerous notable trees, including the Franklinia tree the Bartrams rescued from extinction, and one of the oldest ginkgoes on the continent. Don't miss the historic cider mill carved into stone on the waterfront, which lets you imagine how they pressed apples long ago. Admission is free, but donations are encouraged.

## 92 BOWMAN'S HILL WILDFLOWER PRESERVE

**1635 River Road**
**New Hope, PA 18938; 215-862-2924**
**bhwp.org**
***Wheelchair accessible.***

If you are a lover of spring ephemeral flowers, then Bowman's Hill Wildflower Preserve would make a fantastic day trip. Ephemerals are understory, native flowers that pop up for just a short time each spring. And Bowman's is carpeted with them, including Virginia bluebells, wood poppies, trilliums, and more. Located in New Hope, the site has 5 miles of woodland walking trails, a small pond, and a burbling creek. It's tranquil and magical. One of my favorite spots is the moss garden, which has charming tiny bluet flowers. If woodland fairies and sprites do exist, I bet they hang out here. If you go, be sure to stop at the nursery, with an array of native plants and trees for sale. There's a fee to enter, but check the website for occasional free visitor days.

## 93 CHANTICLEER

**786 Church Road**
**Wayne, PA 19087; 610-687-4163**
**chanticleergarden.org**
***Wheelchair accessible paved path.***

Chanticleer refers to itself as "a pleasure garden." The whole place has a romantic feel and a tranquil, peaceful atmosphere where you can stroll the paths, have a picnic, or lounge and enjoy nature. There are tropical plants in the Teacup Garden, while the Gravel Garden has a Mediterranean vibe. The woodlands surround a meandering creek. Unlike many botanical gardens, you won't find signs next to each plant. Chanticleer encourages visitors to chat with its gardeners if you want to know more. There are also plant lists in designated boxes throughout. Artists are welcome to paint on-site Wednesdays through Fridays. The website regularly updates its "what's in bloom," section, for those visitors who want to see specific flowers and plants.

## 94 H.O. SMITH BOTANIC GARDENS & ARBORETUM AT PENN STATE UNIVERSITY FREE

**East Park Avenue and Bigler Road**
**University Park, PA 16802**
**814-865-9118**
**arboretum.psu.edu**
***Wheelchair accessible walkways.***

If you are visiting the area near Penn State's main campus, don't miss your chance to stroll through one of the state's most beautiful gardens. The H.O. Smith Botanic Gardens & Arboretum is located on the sprawling University Park campus. The garden space is manicured and features a children's garden, a rose garden, and a mesmerizing fountain. There's also an overlook, which is a popular wedding venue, with sweeping views of the surrounding ridge and rolling hills. Don't miss the woodland and wildflower trail near the garden, with old-growth trees that will delight you. The gardens are right next to the Palmer Museum of Art (see page 20).

## 95 HERSHEY GARDENS

**170 Hotel Road**
**Hershey, PA 17033; 717-534-3492**
**hersheygardens.org**
***Wheelchair accessible.***

Hershey is a popular travel destination for chocolate lovers, especially those heading to Hershey Park (see page 42). If you're looking for a quiet place to stroll before or after the park scene, or if you are just a lover of plants, check out Hershey Gardens. The 23-acre site started as a small rose garden. Summer is a great time to visit the now-iconic rose garden bursting with thousands of roses. A special treat is the year-round indoor butterfly atrium, with tropical species from around the globe. There's also a children's garden where everyone can cool down with the mist sprayed from a giant Hershey's Kiss. The most peaceful spot is the Japanese garden that has a pond and trickling stream under the shade of sequoias, redwoods, and maples.

## 96 GOODELL GARDENS & HOMESTEAD FREE

**221 Waterford Street**
**Edinboro, PA 16412; 814-734-6699**
**goodellgardens.org**
***Partial wheelchair accessibility. Paths are gravel or grass.***

If you are headed to Presque Isle State Park (see pages 84–85) or Lake Erie, add the Goodell Gardens & Homestead to your list of places to stop. It's a charming site with gardens and historic buildings. The manicured gardens are themed, with a formal Welcome Garden, a Heritage Garden featuring native plants and shrubs, and a pollinator garden. Don't miss a visit to the champion paper birch, or the rare Franklinia tree. The rhododendron collection is breathtaking; check the website for bloom times. Goodell Gardens is a popular site for weddings, and it regularly hosts festivals, so check the calendar of events. Admission is free, but donations are encouraged.

## 97 JENKINS ARBORETUM & GARDENS FREE

**631 Berwyn Baptist Road**
**Devon, PA 19333; 610-647-8870**
**jenkinsarboretum.org**
***Partial wheelchair accessibility on grounds. Education center is wheelchair accessible. Sensory backpacks available.***

Jenkins Arboretum & Gardens are situated in the suburbs of Philadelphia, referred to as the "Main Line." Here you'll find an abundant array of native flowers and plants, along with walking paths around the 48-acre site. The spring blooms are not to be missed, with a vibrant azalea collection, rhododendrons, and tons of spring ephemeral flowers. Check the "Garden Highlights" section of the website for approximate bloom times. A lovely feature of Jenkins is that it works hard at making the gardens accessible to all. Admission is always free, and while many gardens close in the winter months, Jenkins is open so you can enjoy the trees in all their leafless winter splendor.

## 98 LONGWOOD GARDENS

1001 Longwood Road
Kennett Square, PA 19348
610-388-1000
longwoodgardens.org
*Wheelchair accessible.*
*Listening devices available upon request. ASL Interpreters can be booked two weeks prior to visiting.*

Longwood Gardens is a beloved green space that is a destination. You can easily spend a day exploring the 1,100 acres here and still not see everything. The former duPont estate features manicured gardens, conservatories, fountains, and a dazzling holiday light show that visitors flock to each year. The gardens underwent a massive revision in 2024, now open and called "Longwood Reimagined," featuring the new West Conservatory building, a cascade garden, and new landscape features. The hundreds of thousands of lights sparkle and delight each year from November through January. Be prepared for crowds during the holidays and special events. The space is vast, and even when crowded, it's still super enjoyable to take in the gardens.

## 99 MORRIS ARBORETUM & GARDENS

100 East Northwestern Avenue
Philadelphia, PA 19118; 215-247-5777
morrisarboretum.org
*Wheelchair accessible, but landscape is hilly. ADA-approved path.*

While one should not play favorites, I can't resist saying that Morris Arboretum & Gardens is my favorite place in this chapter. It's the state's official arboretum, and it's a stunner any time of year. Children delight in exploring the gardens, as there are always special exhibits geared toward the littles. There's the garden railway, a fairy garden, a human-size bird's nest high atop the trees, and a series of nets for kids on which to climb and scramble. The trees are monumental. Don't miss the iconic katsura tree and the stately grove of dawn redwoods. The rose garden is best in the summer but has cultivars that bloom longer. Visiting the abundant witch hazels in winter will awaken your senses. The two resident swans charm crowds every day.

FERNERY, MORRIS ARBORETUM & GARDENS, PHILADELPHIA

## 100 PHIPPS CONSERVATORY

One Schenley Park
Pittsburgh, PA 15213; 412-622-6914
phipps.conservatory.org
*Wheelchair accessible except for a portion of the west wing. Sensory bags available.*

Phipps Conservatory is a self-described "green oasis" in the heart of Pittsburgh. While there are some outdoor garden spaces, much of the gardens are inside the vast glass conservatory. While many of the gardens on this list are best visited on sunny, warm days, I imagine Phipps is even a great destination on a rainy or cold winter day as you enjoy the indoor tropical plants and water features. The holidays bring lights and special programming. Phipps also prides itself on its growing art collection, with stunning glass sculptures from Dale Chihuly and other artists. Shoppers will also love the carefully curated shop on-site for gifts or home decor.

## 101 PITTSBURGH BOTANIC GARDEN

799 Pinkerton Run Road
Pittsburgh, PA 15071; 412-444-4464
pittsburghbotanicgarden.org
*Wheelchair accessible visitor center. Paths are paved, gravel, or wood chip, so the gardens have all-terrain wheelchairs available to borrow. Contact ahead of time.*

The plants, flowers, and trees of the Allegheny Plateau are the highlight of the Pittsburgh Botanic Garden. Much of the 65 acres of green space is intentionally wild so visitors can experience the beauty of native plants. The Garden of the Five Senses is great for all, but especially so for children. Here they can see, smell, touch, listen, and even play while learning about the benefits of plants. My favorite spot is the Asian Woodland, which is not to be missed. The lotus pond is gorgeous and peaceful; I could sit there all day and watch the dragonflies flitting about. The gardens have a robust programming schedule, for adults and children alike. Check the website for details before your visit.

LOTUS POND, PITTSBURGH BOTANIC GARDEN, PITTSBURGH

## 102 STONELEIGH FREE

1829 East County Line Road
Villanova, PA 19085; 610-353-5587
stoneleighgarden.org
*Wheelchair accessible paths.*

Stoneleigh is a respite from the hustle and bustle of daily life. It's a Natural Lands site and is always free to visit. The site was once a homestead and features beautifully designed garden rooms, each with a different focus and vibe. The Great Lawn leads up to the historic mansion, an architectural beauty. The Catalpa Court features a water garden framed by towering catalpa trees you'll recognize by their huge leaves and bean-like dangling seed pods. A unique feature is the bog garden, located where a swimming pool once existed. The bog garden showcases water-loving plants like pitcher plants and sundews. There's also a meadow and thoughtfully designed spaces to benefit wildlife.

## 103 TYLER ARBORETUM

515 Painter Road
Media, PA 19063; 610-566-9134
tylerarboretum.org
*Wheelchair accessible.*

Tyler Arboretum is a Delaware County gem, not far from Ridley Creek State Park (see page 85). The arboretum spans 650 acres and features hiking trails throughout. The native woodland walk is a cool retreat in the warmer months. My favorite spot here is the Pinetum, which is an arboretum space completely dedicated to pine trees. Nearby is a towering giant sequoia tree, a rarity of its size on the East Coast. Spring brings carpets of Spanish bluebells along with cherry blossoms and magnolias. The more than 1,500 azalea and rhododendron plants explode from April through June in an array of delicate colors. Yellow goldenrod and purple asters explode with color in early autumn, and the evergreens are a welcome splash of green in the winter.

TYLER ARBORETUM, MEDIA

BALDWIN'S BOOK BARN, WEST CHESTER

**When you walk into a bookstore, you open yourself to new worlds.**

It's no surprise that I love to travel, and everywhere I go I'm always on the hunt for independent bookstores. There's something so lovely about finding a new-to-me bookstore and discovering literary treasures. Old-fashioned bookstores evoke feelings of nostalgia no online shopping experience could ever elicit. We tip our hats to their commitment to the bookstore experience and encourage you to visit and shop at as many independent bookstores as you can from this list. Each bookstore has its own personality, and you're guaranteed to find your next great read.

*Welcome to*

# INDEPENDENT BOOKSTORES

*Find out more about*

# INDEPENDENT BOOKSTORES

## 104 A NOVEL IDEA

**1726 East Passyunk Avenue**
**Philadelphia, PA 19148; 267-764-1202**
**anovelideaphilly.com**

The focus of A Novel Idea is building community around a shared love of books. The bookshop is located in the hip neighborhood of Passyunk (see page 114), which has tons of shops, restaurants, and bars. This bookstore opened its doors in 2018 and survived the pandemic. They love to host events and regular author readings, book club meetings, tarot card readings, storytime, and workshops. If they don't have what you are looking for in stock, they are happy to order it for you.

## 105 AARON'S BOOKS

**35 East Main Street**
**Lititz, PA 17543; 717-627-1990**
**aaronsbooks.com**

Lititz is an adorable town in Pennsylvania Dutch Country. Aaron's Books fits perfectly in the area, which exudes charm. Stroll along Main Street, and you'll find lots of shops, restaurants, and loads of history. The bookstore is larger than it appears from the street and has a great variety of books. The staff is helpful, and their reviews are peppered throughout the store, helping you find your next great read. They also have a small selection of gift items for the booklovers on your shopping list. After you visit the store, grab a warm and delicious pretzel from nearby Julius Sturgis Pretzels (see page 74) and you will be in heaven.

## 106 BALDWIN'S BOOK BARN

**865 Lenape Road**
**West Chester, PA 19382; 610-696-0816**
**bookbarn.com**

Baldwin's Book Barn in West Chester is a road-trip-worthy bookstore that specializes in used and rare books. You'll love the rustic charm of the bookstore as you explore all of its nooks filled with books. Prepare to spend a couple of hours looking through the shelves that span many rooms and floors. I bet you'll discover more than one book that you didn't know you needed. The building was built in 1822, and the natural wood throughout is super cozy. They also have maps and prints for sale and are eager to help you track down literary treasures.

## 107 BIG BLUE MARBLE BOOKSTORE

**551 Carpenter Lane**
**Philadelphia, PA 19119; 215-844-1870**
**bigbluemarblebooks.com**

Big Blue Marble Bookshop is a neighborhood favorite, located a few doors down from the well-loved Mount Airy Co-op, a small grocery store. The bookstore is on the smaller side but has a carefully curated inventory. The bookshop loves to feature books by local authors, usually displaying their books in the front of the store. They have cute gift items and a great children's section. One of the best parts of the bookshop is its super-cozy upstairs reading room, which is always stocked with tea. If you are looking for a bookstore where you can sneak away and hide for a few hours, Big Blue Marble might fit the bill.

## 108 THE BOOK TRADER

**7 North 2nd Street**
**Philadelphia, PA 19106; 215-925-2080**
**phillybooktrader.com**

I'm old enough to remember when The Book Trader was on South Street. I used to love going there in my college days to spend hours among the stacks of used books. The store has been a Philadelphia staple for nearly 50 years, now located in historic Old City. Prepare to be a little overwhelmed on your first visit because the bookstore has books everywhere. It's the kind of place to go when you aren't sure what you're looking for, but you'll know it when you see it. You can easily spend a few hours looking through the offerings, spread across shelves, rooms, and several floors. It's also a great place to find vintage books. I guarantee that you will leave happy with your finds.

INSIDE SIGN AT THE BOOK TRADER, PHILADELPHIA

## 109 CARROLL & CARROLL BOOKSELLERS

**740 Main Street**
**Stroudsburg, PA 18360; 570-420-1516**
**carroll-carroll-booksellers.hub.biz**

The Pocono Mountain region is a popular day trip area for nature lovers. If you find yourself in the Northeastern part of the state, you won't regret adding a stop at the charming Carroll & Carroll Booksellers. The shop is located on Main Street in the heart of East Stroudsburg. It sells new, used, and rare books. While it doesn't have much of a web presence, don't let that stop you from visiting to see what you might find hiding in plain sight on the shelves. The store has an abundance of mysteries and thrillers, and the staff is super helpful.

## 110 CITY OF ASYLUM BOOKSTORE

**40 West North Avenue**
**Pittsburgh, PA 15212; 412-435-1112**
**cityofasylumbooks.org**

This women-run independent bookstore in Pittsburgh's Northside neighborhood is so unique. It has a wide selection of international and translated titles in addition to the normal bookstore offerings. There's a large, open space with a performance stage and grand piano, so it's no surprise that regular events like jazz and story slams are hosted here. I was impressed by the poetry book offerings, which many bookstores tend to skimp on. The bookstore's name comes from a movement created to support writers persecuted for their writings. The bookstore also operates a nonprofit organization that supports exiled writers and advocates for freedom of expression.

## 111 CLAY BOOKSTORE

**2450 West Main Street**
**Ephrata, PA 17522; 717-733-7253**
**justplainbusiness.com/clay-book-store**

The Clay Bookstore is an unassuming Christian bookstore in Ephrata. They have a huge inventory of Bibles and Christian reading, in addition to a variety of homeschooling supplies. Maps and nature books are also well-represented in this family-run bookshop. It doesn't have much of a web presence, but the staff is friendly and will help you find what you are looking for. It's located close to the Historic Ephrata Cloister (see page 33), the Railroad Museum of Pennsylvania (see page 94), and Pennsylvania Dutch Country shopping (see page 113) in Lancaster and surrounding towns.

## DOYLESTOWN BOOKSHOP

**16 South Main Street**
**Doylestown, PA 18901; 215-230-7610**
**doylestownbookshop.com/store/1**

I could easily spend hours in the Doylestown Bookshop. It's located in the heart of the downtown Doylestown shopping district (see page 111) close to the James A. Michener Art Museum (see page 19) and the Mercer Museum (see page 34). The store is huge and is bursting with books from many different genres. They have a great children's section and have so many adorable gift offerings. The store itself is road-trip worthy, but being close to so many other sites, you can easily spend an entire day in this charming Bucks County town. Its sister bookstore is the Lahaska Bookshop in nearby Peddler's Village. The staff are friendly and eager to help you track down books on your list.

## 113 FIREFLY BOOKSTORE

**271 West Main Street**
**Kutztown, PA 19530; 484-648-2712**
**fireflybookstore.com**

The Firefly Bookstore is a lovely shop just steps away from Kutztown University of Pennsylvania. You'll know you're there when you see the bright-pink façade. The walkable downtown area has a variety of shops and restaurants with a great college-town vibe. The bookstore sells new and used books and an impressive assortment of board games. Its children's book selection is sizable, and there's a separate section featuring books by local authors. The shop also sells gifts, notebooks, stationery, calendars, and puzzles. Plan to spend at least an hour digging through the shelves to see everything. Firefly regularly hosts book events like author readings and signings.

## 114 GORDONVILLE BOOK STORE

**275 Old Leacock Road**
**Gordonville, PA 17529; 717-768-3512**
**advkeen.co/gordonvillebkstre**

The Gordonville Book Store is a small, Amish-owned-and-operated bookstore. It has a very limited web presence, so you'll just have to pop in to see what's in stock. The bookshop has a variety of religious and children's books, in addition to some great Amish cookbooks, tons of homeschooling supplies, and art and crafts supplies. The bookshop is very quaint, with limited signage. Scrapbooking supplies and rustic home decor items round out the store's offerings. It's located near Lancaster and Pennsylvania Dutch shopping (see page 113).

## 115 HAKIM'S BOOKSTORE

**210 South 52nd Street**
**Philadelphia, PA 19139; 215-474-9495**
**hakimsbookstore.com**

Hakim's Bookstore is the oldest Black-owned bookshop in Philadelphia. The late Dawud Hakim, founder and namesake, opened the shop in 1959. Hakim's mission was to provide books that focused on African American history and culture, which were hard to come by at the time. Hakim's filled the gap and soon became a vital meeting spot. Hakim's daughters and granddaughter now run the historic shop, which even has its own historical marker. They still specialize in curating a great selection of books by and for African Americans, in addition to cool Afrocentric gifts. Hakim's also hosts events and community gatherings.

## 116 HARRIET'S BOOKSHOP

**258 East Girard Avenue**
**Philadelphia, PA 19125; 267-241-2617**
**oursisterbookshops.com**

Harriet's Bookshop and its owner, Jeannine Cook, were featured in Oprah's online magazine, *Oprah Daily*. The unique Philadelphia bookstore prides itself on featuring and curating the creative works of "women authors, artists, and activists." Named in honor of Harriet Tubman, the store is one of three sister shops. Harriet's is more than a bookstore; it's an art gallery, an event space, and a center for community connection. It's located in the Fishtown neighborhood of Philadelphia, along the Frankford Avenue shopping district (see page 111). Harriet's also has a lovely selection of merchandise celebrating Black women authors and poets.

## 117 LAHASKA BOOKSHOP

**162 A Route 263 Peddler's Village**
**Lahaska, PA 18931; 267-544-5131**
**doylestownbookshop.com/store/2**

The Lahaska Bookshop is the sister bookstore to the Doylestown Bookshop, both located in Bucks County. The Lahaska Bookshop is in Peddler's Village (see page 114), which is a popular and picturesque shopping area near New Hope (see pages 113–114). Much like its sister store, the Lahaska Shop has a wide variety of books, games, toys, and other adorable gift items.

## 118 MAIN POINT BOOKS

**116 North Wayne Avenue**
**Wayne, PA 19087; 484-580-6978**
**mainpointbooks.com**

Main Point Books is the go-to bookstore in Philadelphia's affluent suburbs known as "the Main Line." The bookshop is small but mighty and is a hub for local authors and community literary gatherings. If the store doesn't have what you need in stock, the staff will track it down for you. A busy event calendar features signings and readings by local authors. The shop also hosts regular book club meetings. It has a cute selection of bookish gift items alongside its carefully curated book selection.

HARRIET'S BOOKSHOP, PHILADELPHIA

## 119 MIDTOWN SCHOLAR BOOKSTORE

**1302 North 3rd Street**
**Harrisburg, PA 17102; 717-236-1680**
**midtownscholar.com**

Midtown Scholar Bookstore is a huge space, which can be a little overwhelming (in a good way) when you walk in. There are literally shelves upon shelves of new and used books, so plan to spend a fair amount of time hunting for treasures. There's a café and cozy seating throughout the store. The bookshop is located in a building that was originally a movie theater, became a department store, and is now a bookstore with hundreds of thousands of titles. It's located just blocks away from the Pennsylvania State Capitol complex (see page 10), so if you are heading to Harrisburg and are a lover of books, make it a point to stop by Midtown Scholar.

## 120 MORAVIAN BOOKSHOP

**428 Main Street**
**Bethlehem, PA 18018; 888-661-2888**
**moravian.edu/bookshop**

The original Moravian Bookshop opened in 1745, making it the oldest bookstore in the country, and one of the oldest in the world. It operated independently until 2018 when Moravian University took it over. The bookshop is now the student bookstore for Moravian University, and Barnes & Noble manages the daily operations. The store is still home to a huge selection of books detailing the history of the area, including books about Moravians and industrial history. Moravian Bookshop is located in the heart of Bethlehem, which was once a major hub for industry, particularly Bethlehem Steel. The store also sells gift items in addition to its collection of new books.

MIDTOWN SCHOLAR BOOKSTORE, HARRISBURG

## Famous Authors from Pennsylvania

Pennsylvania has no shortage of famous authors who were either born in the Keystone State or wrote here. In fact, the list is quite long, so what follows is a list of some of the most famous authors and their connection to Pennsylvania.

**Edward Abbey** The author and environmentalist born in Indiana, PA, often wrote about the American West. His novel, *The Monkey Wrench Gang*, was probably his most famous book.

**Louisa May Alcott** The author of *Little Women* was born in the Germantown section of Philadelphia.

**Stan & Jan Berenstain** The married couple were both born in Philadelphia. They wrote and illustrated the *Berenstain Bears* series of children's books.

**Pearl S. Buck** Although she was not born in PA, Pearl S. Buck lived in Perkasie for about 40 years and is buried there. Best known for her novel, *The Good Earth*, she was the recipient of both a Pulitzer Prize and a Nobel Prize in Literature.

**Rachel Carson** A scientist by trade, Rachel Carson is often credited with starting the environmental movement when she published her book, *Silent Spring*. She was born near Pittsburgh where you can visit her homestead.

**Dean R. Koontz** Hugely popular horror science-fiction writer Dean R. Koontz was born in Pennsylvania and graduated from Shippensburg University. His books have sold more than 500 million copies.

**James A. Michener** Doylestown native, James A. Michener, is well known for his lengthy, place-based historical fiction. He won the Pulitzer Prize for his first novel, *Tales of the South Pacific*. His multi-million dollar donation helped establish the James A. Michener Art Museum (see page 19).

**Edgar Allan Poe** One of America's most well-known horror and suspense writers, Edgar Allan Poe wrote most of his works in Philadelphia. You can visit the home where he lived. The Edgar Allan Poe National Historic Site is in Philadelphia (see page 19).

**John Updike** Two-time Pulitzer winner, John Updike was born and raised in Pennsylvania. He wrote more than 60 books. His childhood home is now a museum and listed on the U.S. National Register of Historic Places.

**Jennifer Weiner** The bestselling author moved to Philadelphia in 1994 to work for the Philadelphia Inquirer and decided to stay in the city. Her books have sold millions of copies.

**August Wilson** Pittsburgh native son August Wilson was a two-time Pulitzer Prize winner for his plays, *Fences* and *The Piano Lesson.* He dedicated his life to writing about the African-American Experience. The August Wilson African American Cultural Center (see page 31) is named in his honor.

## 121 OPEN BOOK BOOKSTORE

**7900 High School Road**
**Elkins Park, PA 19027; 267-627-4888**
**openbookphilly.com**

Open Book Bookstore is a small neighborhood bookshop in Elkins Park, a suburb of Philadelphia. The owner is a former literary agent, editor, and author, so she makes excellent recommendations. The shop regularly hosts themed book events and author signings. It has a nicely curated selection of books, including children's and young adult books. Open Book Bookstore also has a number of books by authors based in the Greater Philadelphia area.

## 122 THE OTTO BOOKSTORE

**107 West Fourth Street**
**Williamsport, PA 17701; 570-326-5764**
**ottobookstore.com**

The Otto Bookstore is one of the oldest independently owned and operated bookstores in the country. The bookstore opened in 1841 and has been part of the Williamsport community ever since. The newest owners took over in 2017 and have continued the indie tradition. The bookshop calls itself "a booklover's paradise," and that description is spot on. From tons of books to bookish gifts, you can easily lose yourself among the shelves of this neighborhood staple. The shop also has regular author events and children's story time.

## 123 RIVERSTONE BOOKS

**123A**
**8850 Covenant Avenue**
**Pittsburgh, PA 15237; 412-366-1001**

**123B**
**5841 Forbes Avenue**
**Pittsburgh, PA 15217; 412-422-2220**
**riverstonebookstore.com**

Riverstone Books calls itself the largest independent bookstore in Pittsburgh. It's got two locations—the original shop is the McCandless Crossing location (Covenant Avenue), while the Squirrel Hill location opened more recently. Riverstone sells new books in many genres, including popular and literary fiction, nonfiction, and children's books. They also carry children's games and toys, as well as gifts and greeting cards. The staff are super friendly and always eager to help you find your next great read or the perfect gift. Both Riverstone shops have a busy calendar, with weekly story time for the little ones, as well as book club meetings and other events.

## 124 THE SQUIRREL & ACORN BOOKSHOP

**103 South Allen Street**
**State College, PA 16801; 814-699-9018**
**thesquirrelandacornbookshop.com**

The Squirrel & Acorn Bookshop has the most adorable name for an indie bookstore. Located in State College just minutes from Penn State (and the Palmer Museum of Art (see page 20) and H.O. Botanic Gardens (see page 52), this cute and cozy store has a curated selection of new books. What's unique about this shop is its selection of writing tools. It offers a lovely variety of fountain pens and a rainbow of colored inks. It also has pencils and paper for all of your old-fashioned writing needs. There are comfy spots to sit and read too.

## 125 WHISTLESTOP BOOKSHOP

**129 West High Street**
**Carlisle, PA 17013; 717-243-4744**
**whistlestoppers.com**

Whistlestop Bookshop is located in the heart of Carlisle, just steps away from Dickinson College. A friendly bookstore cat may greet you upon entry. This bookshop sells new books and has a great selection of fiction and nonfiction, including children's books. The store also offers a plethora of cards, music, puzzles, toys, games, journals, and bookish gifts like T-shirts and totes. The store also hosts events such as author readings and has a robust web presence, so you can check out inventory before you head there. As indie bookstores often do, Whistlestop can order a book for you if it's not in stock.

## 126 WHITE WHALE BOOKSTORE

**4754 Liberty Avenue**
**Pittsburgh, PA 15224; 412-224-2847**
**whitewhalebookstore.com**

The first thing I noticed when I walked into White Whale Bookstore in Pittsburgh was the abundance of staff picks and reviews popping out all over. I love bookstores that have staff recommendations like this. The bookshop is in a great location, near many other day trip spots (like Lawrenceville see page 113, Phipps Conservatory see page 54, the Pittsburgh Zoo see page 26, and the Frick see page 33). It has a huge variety of new books and an adorably decorated children's section. Helpful and friendly staff can help you find your next great read.

OLD BOOKS AT A VINTAGE BOOKSTORE

## The beer scene in Pennsylvania is one of the best in the country.

When planning Philadelphia, William Penn originally said he would allow no taverns or alehouses. Fortunately, he had a change of heart and the people got brewing. Today the state is home to the oldest brewery in the nation, D.G. Yuengling & Son (see page 77), and is a top beer producer. People come from all over the nation for events or to experience one of the many taprooms or brewpubs. So whether you love a pilsner, a hearty ale, or want to sample it all, Pennsylvania has something for you.

Welcome to

# BREWERIES

## 127 EAST END BREWERY

**127A**
147 Julius Street
Pittsburgh PA 15206; 412-537-2337

**127B**
651 Washington Road
Mount Lebanon, PA 15228
eastendbrewing.com

## 128 LANCASTER BREWING COMPANY

**128A**
302 North Plum Street
Lancaster, PA 17602; 717-391-6258

**128B**
469 Eisenhower Boulevard
Harrisburg, PA 17111; 717-564-4448

**128C**
2323 Lincoln Highway East
Lancaster, PA 17602; 717-826-9555
lancasterbrewing.com

## 129 PHILADELPHIA BREWING COMPANY

2440 Frankford Avenue
Philadelphia, PA 19125; 215-427-2739
philadelphiabrewing.com

## 130 SLY FOX BREWING

**130A**
331 Circle of Progress Drive
Pottstown, PA 19464; 484-300-4644

**130B**
520 Kimberton Road
Phoenixville, PA 19460; 610-935-4540

**130C**
820 Knitting Mills Way, #100
Wyomissing, PA 19610; 484-878-2154

**130D**
20 Liberty Boulevard, Suite 100
Malvern, PA 19355; 484-328-3567

**130E**
46 South 4th Street
Pittsburgh, PA 15219; 412-815-4955

**130F**
300 Liberty Avenue, Suite 100
Pittsburgh, PA 15222; 412-586-7474
slyfoxbeer.com

## 131 TROEGS

200 East Hershey Park Drive
Hershey, PA 17033; 717-534-1297
troegs.com

## 132 VICTORY BREWING

**132A**
420 Acorn Lane
Downingtown, PA 19335; 610-873-0881

**132B**
3127 Lower Valley Road
Parkesburg, PA 19365; 484-718-5080

**132C**
1776 Benjamin Franklin Parkway
Philadelphia, PA 19103; 445-223-1130

**132D**
650 West Cypress Street, Kennett Square, PA 19348; 484-730-1870
victorybeer.com

## 133 WEYERBACHER

518 Bank Street
Emmaus, PA 18049; 610-438-3888
weyerbacher.combeer flightbeer flight

MALE SOMMELIER POURING RED WINE

**William Penn planted some of the earliest known wine grapes in Pennsylvania in 1863.**

The commercial wine industry in Pennsylvania can trace its roots back to Pierre Legaux's Pennsylvania Vine Company, opened in 1787. Today, enthusiasts can enjoy the many outstanding wine bars, vineyards, and winemakers along the banks of the Schuykill River. This list is just a small taste of all of Pennsylvania's wineries.

*Welcome to*

# WINERIES

## 134 ADAMS COUNTY WINERY

251 Peach Tree Road
Orrtanna, PA 17353; 717-334-4631
adamscountywinery.com

## 135 BLUE RIDGE ESTATE & WINERY

239 Blue Ridge Road
Saylorsburg, PA 18353; 610-895-4205
blueridgeestatewinery.com

## 136 CHADDSFORD WINERY

632 Baltimore Pike
Chadds Ford, PA 19317; 610-388-6221
chaddsford.com

## 137 CROSSING VINEYARDS & WINERY

1853 Wrightstown Road
Newtown, PA 18940; 215-493-6500
crossingvineyards.com

## 138 GALEN GLEN WINERY

255 Winter Mountain Drive
Andreas, PA 18211; 570-386-3682
galenglen.com

## 139 MAZZA VINEYARDS

11815 East Lake Road
North East, PA 16428; 800-796-9463
enjoymazza.com

## 140 MOUNT HOPE ESTATE & WINERY

2775 Lebanon Road
Manheim, PA 17545; 717-665-7021
mounthope.estate

## 141 PENNS WOODS WINERY

124 Beaver Valley Road
Chadds Ford, PA 19317
610-459-0808
pennswoodswinery.com

JULIUS STURGIS PRETZEL BAKERY, LITITZ

## Pennsylvania was a central force in the Industrial Revolution.

Pennsylvania's largest city, Philadelphia, was once known as the "workshop of the world," where manufacturing thrived. Alas, Pennsylvania, like many places across the country, is not the manufacturing behemoth it once was. But there are still many places where Made in America means Made in Pennsylvania. Many places don't invite the public inside to see behind the curtain, but the few locations in this chapter still do. They want you to see how they craft their products, and they hope you will buy them and tell your friends to buy them too.

# Welcome to MADE IN PENNSYLVANIA

## *Find out more about*
# MADE IN PENNSYLVANIA

### 142 HERR'S SNACK FACTORY

271 Old Baltimore Pike
Nottingham, PA 19362
800-284-7488
herrs.com/visit-us/
*Wheelchair accessible.*

I love crunchy, salty snacks. I mean, who doesn't?! Herr's is one of my go-to snack makers, so it's fun to go behind the scenes to see how everything is made. Herr's makes potato chips, pretzels, popcorn, cheese curls, and tortilla strips. You'll take a guided tour through the factory, watch some videos to learn about the company's history, and, of course, have an opportunity to stock up on snacks in the store. The tour isn't offered every day, so make sure the factory is open on the day of your visit and buy tickets ahead of time. Each tour is limited to only 15 people.

### 143 HERSHEY'S CHOCOLATE WORLD

101 Chocolate World Way
Hershey, PA 17033; 717-534-4900
chocolateworld.com
*Wheelchair accessible. Certified Autism Center. Scheduled sensory-friendly hours. Detailed allergy information available on website.*

Hershey's Chocolate is iconic. No s'more is complete without it. And this huge company was founded right here in Pennsylvania. There's a whole city named after Milton Hershey. Separate from Hershey Park (see page 42), but just steps away, you'll find Hershey's Chocolate World. Entrance to the Chocolate Tour ride is free, but to see and do everything else costs an extra fee. The tour will educate you on how cocoa beans become chocolate bars. Other chocolate-themed things to do here include a choose-your-own-adventure theater experience, a chocolate-tasting journey, an opportunity to design and make your own candy bar or stuff a customized 1-pound Reese's peanut butter cup with your choice of ingredients.

### 144 JULIUS STURGIS PRETZEL BAKERY

219 East Main Street
Lititz, PA 17543; 717-626-4354
juliussturgis.com
*Wheelchair accessible.*

Julius Sturgis opened America's first pretzel factory in 1861, and the company has been making pretzels ever since. While the company's production has moved elsewhere, you can still tour the original pretzel bakery, which is now a historic landmark. Look for the giant pretzel outside, and you'll know you're in the right place. You can even try your hand at rolling out and twisting pretzels using a flour-and-water mixture. The pretzel twisting is just for practice, but you can buy a warm-and-chewy soft pretzel in the store. They are absolutely delicious. The bakery is located in Lititz, in the heart of Pennsylvania Dutch Country.

POTATO CHIP FACTORY

## 145 MARTIN GUITAR FACTORY

**510 Sycamore Street**
**Nazareth, PA 18064; 610-759-2837**
**advkeen.co/martinfactory**
***Wheelchair accessible.***

Martin guitars are legendary. Some of the biggest names in music history have played Martin guitars, including Hank Williams, Elvis Presley, Bob Dylan, and too many others to name. You can visit the factory to witness first-hand how these beautiful guitars are made. The tour size is limited to eight people per tour, but there are multiple tours each weekday. It is best to buy tickets ahead of time. There's also a free museum, but donations are suggested. At the Pickin' Parlor, you can even play some sought-after guitars, which are rotated regularly, so you never know what you might get to strum.

## 146 MOKA ORIGINS FREE

**952 Bethany Turnpike**
**Honesdale, PA 18431; 570-979-1010**
**mokaorigins.com**
***Wheelchair accessible.***

The makers at Moka Origins pride themselves on sourcing sustainable and ethical cocoa and coffee beans. The result is out-of-this-world chocolate and coffee. Located on the campus of the Himalayan Institute (see page 104), Moka runs a small factory and store. On Saturdays, you can learn how the chocolate is made and enjoy samples. You can also book a paid private tour if you want to visit on another day. The tour and tasting lasts about 45 minutes, but you will wish it lasted longer. You can stock up on chocolate and coffee at the store or sign up for a subscription.

## 147 U.S. MINT FREE

**151 North Independence Mall East**
**Philadelphia, PA 19106; 215-408-0110**
**advkeen.co/usmint**
***Wheelchair accessible.***

There are only three mints in the country, and one is located in Philadelphia. In fact, the country's very first mint was in Philly, just steps away from where it is today. The weekdays-only tour is self-guided and free. Spring and summer months bring hordes of visitors to this historic neighborhood, so there may be a line if you are visiting at these popular times. Coin production doesn't happen every day, so there's a chance you may not see machines in action on your visit. An extra treat comes in the form of seven huge Tiffany glass mosaics that are stunning. If you are a numismatist, don't miss the gift shop where you can buy all kinds of coins.

## 148 YARDS BREWING COMPANY

**500 Spring Garden Street**
**Philadelphia, PA 19123; 215-525-0175**
**yardsbrewing.com/pages/tours**
***Wheelchair accessible.***

Yards beer is a Philadelphia staple. The brewery celebrated 30 years of brewing in 2024 and is still going strong. Once a day on weekdays, and more frequently on weekends, Yards offers tours explaining how its beers goes from "grain to glass." The tour is adults-only, and your ticket fee gets you a sample brew. You'll feel oh-so-small as you walk by the gigantic equipment where all the magic happens. Tour sizes are limited to 15 people, so I'd book a ticket ahead of time. Afterward, the brewpub has all its beers on tap, along with tasty bites.

## 149 D.G. YUENGLING & SON, INC. FREE

420 Mahantongo Street
Pottsville, PA 17901; 570-628-4890
yuengling.com/visit-us/
*Tour is not wheelchair accessible.*

In Pennsylvania, you can walk into many bars, order a lager, and the bartender will instinctively hand you a bottle of Yuengling. The tour at D.G. Yuengling & Son, Inc., starts off with a visit to the historic, hand-dug caves where the first kegs of beer chilled before being tapped. As you continue on, you'll head over to see the modern-day production of the oldest brewery still operating in the country. The tour is free and family-friendly, but you must have a valid ID to sample or buy beer. The tour schedule changes throughout the year, so check the website ahead of your visit. It's important to note that you must wear closed-toed shoes to take the tour.

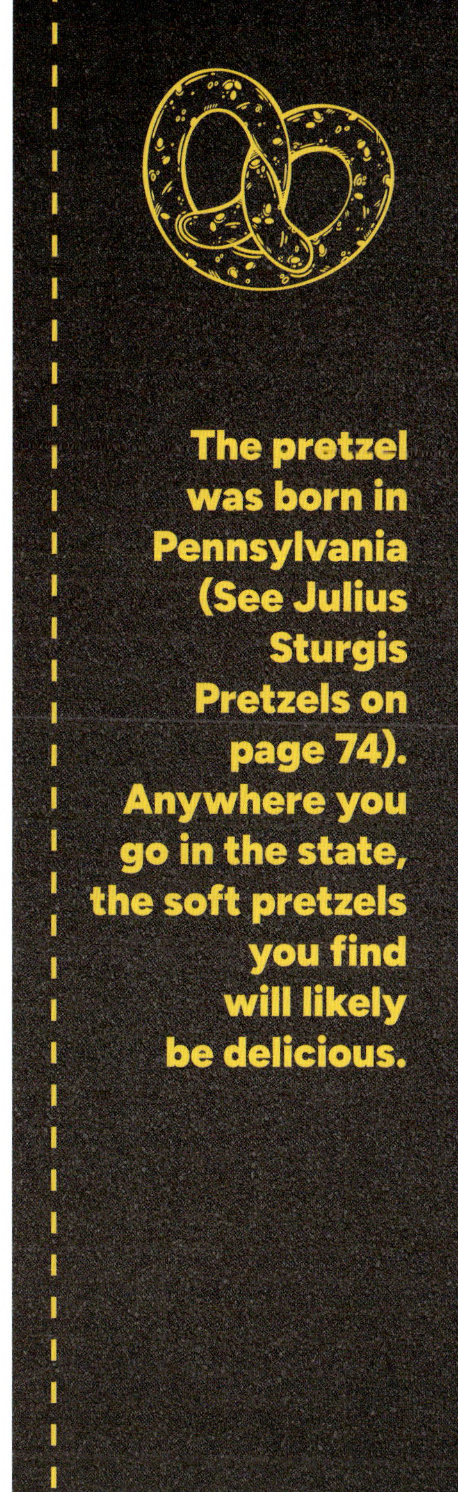

SHORELINE VIEW OF PRESQUE ISLE STATE PARK, ERIE

**Pennsylvania is an outdoor lover's paradise.**

There are endless opportunities to explore mountains, lakes, rolling hills, amazing vistas, and dense forests. Adventure awaits those who love hiking, walking, boating, biking, or just being outside and connecting with the living Earth. **Warning:** Hunting is allowed at many of these locations, so it's vital that you wear blaze-orange clothing if you are visiting during hunting season. I've provided reminders for places where hunting is popular, but it's important to check the website of any outdoor area before visiting to ensure safe travel.

# Welcome to OUTDOOR ADVENTURES

**Pennsylvania has 124 state parks, amounting to 300,000 acres of outdoor space in addition to state and federal forests.**

*Find out more about*

# OUTDOOR ADVENTURES

## 150 ALLEGHENY NATIONAL FOREST FREE

4 Farm Colony Drive
Warren, PA 16365; 814-723-5150
fs.usda.gov/Allegheny
*Several wheelchair accessible trails. Call for more details.*

The Allegheny National Forest is huge, covering more than 500,000 acres in the northwestern corner of the state. The best way to explore is to do some research ahead of time and have a destination in mind. No matter where you land, you'll be greeted by mountains, towering trees, and stunning vistas. Great spots to check out include the Hearts Content Scenic Area, Rimrock Overlook, and the Tionesta Creek area. Hearts Content features stunning old-growth hemlock and white pine trees. There's an interpretive trail and picnic area at this spot where some trees have lived for hundreds of years. Rimrock Overlook has great views of Kinzua Bay. And, if you visit the Tionesta Creek area on July evenings, chances are you will get to see the stunning light show the synchronous fireflies put on every year. Hunting is allowed seasonally, so be sure to wear orange if exploring during that time.

## 151 BEAR CREEK PRESERVE FREE

47 Rabbit Run Lane
Wilkes-Barre Township, PA 18702
610-353-5587
natlands.org/bear-creek-preserve
*Not wheelchair accessible.*

Bear Creek Preserve is a hidden gem in the heart of the Pocono Mountains. It's a refuge for abundant wildlife, including black bears, coyotes, and foxes. The Natural Lands preserve is nearly 4,000 acres, larger than many state parks. Natural Lands is a nonprofit organization that preserves green space in Pennsylvania and New Jersey. There are two separate sections at the Bear Creek Preserve, but the address given here takes you to the larger location. The land is gorgeous year-round, but especially so in May/June when all of the mountain laurel is in bloom, covering the forest in a gorgeous pink blanket. Autumn leaf peeping is also a fantastic time to visit, so monitor the Pennsylvania DCNR's foliage reports if visiting in the fall. Hunting is generally prohibited, except for occasional permit hunting to control the white-tailed deer population. Check the website before you go and always wear blaze orange if you are in the woods during hunting season.

## 152 CALEDONIA STATE PARK FREE

101 Pine Grove Road
Fayetteville, PA 17222; 717-352-2161
advkeen.co/CalendoniaPark
*ADA-accessible swimming pool, picnic area, campground, cabins, a fishing pier, and visitor center.*

If you're looking to experience the Blue Ridge Mountains without heading too far south, consider a trip to Caledonia State Park. The 1,125-acre park stretches between Adams and Franklin

Counties and is the northernmost point of the Blue Ridge Mountains. There are 10 miles of hiking trails throughout the park, ranging from steep and difficult to flat and easy. Another key feature of the park is that you can walk a small slice of the Appalachian Trail. Anglers will enjoy fishing for trout at several park waterways. Small game and deer hunting are also allowed seasonally throughout a large section of the park, so wear blaze orange if visiting during hunting season. There's also a public golf course and picnic pavilions, perfect for a day trip.

## 153 CHERRY VALLEY NATIONAL WILDLIFE REFUGE FREE

**2138 Croasdale Road**
**Stroudsburg, PA, 18360; 973-702-7266**
**fws.gov/refuge/cherry-valley**
***Paved paths are wheelchair accessible, though some have steep inclines.***

Cherry Valley National Wildlife Refuge was established to provide vital habitat for migrating birds. Visiting in the autumn months is the best opportunity to see migrating raptors, such as hawks. Four miles of the Appalachian Trail bisect the park, along with other hiking trails through the wetland habitat. The site is a former golf course, so the paths are paved and accessible for wheelchairs and strollers. In addition to bird-watching, abundant outdoor opportunities await at this Pocono Mountain refuge, including hunting, fishing, archery, photography, snowshoeing, and cross-country skiing in snowy winters. The refuge is also home to several threatened and endangered species, so it's important to stay on the trails. No dogs (other than service animals) are allowed. Remember to wear blaze orange if visiting during hunting season.

## 154 COOK FOREST STATE PARK FREE

**100 Route 36**
**Cooksburg, PA 16217; 814-744-8407**
**advkeen.co/CookForestPark**
***Wheelchair accessible, roped, sensory trail; paved picnic area.***

Cook Forest State Park has one of the few remaining old-growth forests left in the state. An old-growth forest is one that humans have not significantly altered. Many Pennsylvania forests were clear-cut in the past, so finding old-growth trees is rare across the state. The old-growth section of Cook Forest is called the Forest Cathedral, and it's a magical, mossy forest with towering hemlock and white pine trees. It has been named a National Natural Landmark and is well worth a day trip to visit these majestic old trees. Cook Forest is a whopping 8,500 acres and offers a long list of outdoor adventures. The Clarion River runs through the park and is a popular spot for tubing in the summer months. This park also has spaces for a variety of winter sports options, including cross-country skiing, sledding, and ice-skating. There are also biking trails and several picnic pavilions. Hunting is allowed seasonally, so be mindful of that when deciding when to explore.

## 155 DELAWARE WATER GAP NATIONAL RECREATION AREA FREE

**1978 River Road**
**Bushkill, PA 18324; 570-426-2452**
**nps.gov/dewa**
***Accessible trails, overlooks, visitor centers.***

Delaware Water Gap National Recreation Area is a national treasure right in our backyard. The name comes from the gap the Delaware River carved into the mountains eons ago. The park is incredibly popular, and since it's close to many urban spaces, it can get crowded during summer weekends. The earlier you get to the park in those peak times, the better chance you'll have at getting a parking spot and access. Mt. Minsi, Mt. Tammany, and the waterfalls are the most popular places, but there are 150 miles of trails throughout the park. In addition to spectacular vistas, there are many things to do, from paddling the Delaware River to hiking, fishing, and hunting. Wildlife abounds in this park—on a recent visit, I spotted numerous bald eagles, and a black bear, and I heard coyotes off in the distance. Hunting is permitted, so wear orange if visiting during hunting season.

## 156 ERIE NATIONAL WILDLIFE REFUGE FREE

**11296 Wood Duck Lane**
**Guys Mills, PA 16327; 814-580-9983**
**fws.gov/refuge/erie**
***Accessible trail, observation platforms, visitor center.***

Erie National Wildlife Refuge is made up of two separate places. The address here will take you to the park headquarters and the Sugar Lake Division, where there's access to the Tsuga Trail. This trail is great for hiking in the warmer months or cross-country skiing and snowshoeing in the winter. The nearby Seneca Division is mainly wetlands, but it has two designated trails. The Trolley Line Trail is a great place to spot spring ephemeral flowers—those beautiful but fleeting woodland flowers only in bloom in April and May. Look for trout lilies, red trillium, or my favorite, jack-in-the-pulpit. The wetlands make some of this section tough to access, so always check with the park office about conditions. The refuge also has kid-focused programming. Hunting is permitted, so wear blaze orange during hunting season.

## 157 GREAT ALLEGHENY PASSAGE FREE

**P.O. Box 228**
**Homestead, PA 15120**
**gaptrail.org**
***Wheelchair accessible sections with one longer 19-mile portion.***

If you are an avid cyclist, the Great Allegheny Passage is probably on your bucket list. If you enjoy exploring the countryside by bicycle, the GAP trail might make a great series of day trips. The mostly flat, crushed limestone trail starts in Maryland and winds its way through Western PA before ending in Pittsburgh. It passes through about a dozen trail towns with restaurants and shops. It also follows the shorelines of three rivers: the Casselman, the Youghiogheny, and the Monongahela. A part of the trail weaves its way through Ohiopyle State Park (see page 131), which has stunning rapids and waterfalls. The website has great info to help you plan your ride. About a million people visit the GAP trail each year. Note that hunting is allowed along various parts of the trail, so if you are adventuring during hunting season, wear visible orange.

## 158 JOHN HEINZ NATIONAL WILDLIFE REFUGE FREE

**8601 Lindbergh Boulevard**
**Philadelphia, PA 19153; 215-365-3118**
**fws.gov/refuge/john-heinz-tinicum**
***Wheelchair accessible trails, visitor center, fishing platform.***

Thousands of people zip past the John Heinz National Wildlife Refuge daily without realizing that so much nature is close to the Philadelphia International Airport. The refuge was the first urban wildlife refuge in the country. It's a fantastic spot for a hike or bike ride, and the bird-watching is stellar. Birds stop here to refuel on their journey through the Atlantic Flyway, a migratory route. Early fall also brings tons of migrating monarch butterflies. There are a few boardwalks that allow you to feel like you are floating above the water. Great signage throughout helps guide and inform visitors. You'll be so immersed in nature you might not notice all the airplanes taking off and landing nearby. Note: Only archery hunting is allowed at this location, so check the website before a fall or winter visit and wear orange if hunting is permitted the day of your visit.

## 159 LEONARD HARRISON STATE PARK FREE

**4797 Route 660**
**Wellsboro, PA 16901; 570-724-3061**
**advkeen.co/leoharrisonpark**
***Wheelchair accessible trail and overlook area. ADA park office and campground restroom.***

The Grand Canyon of Pennsylvania is on the must-see list of many travelers in the state. For the best views, head to Leonard Harrison State Park, which is located on the east rim of the canyon, also known as Pine Creek Gorge. The park's Overlook Trail offers sweeping vistas of the gorge. The park is popular year-round, but especially so in leaf-peeping season. If you are lucky enough to visit from late September through the middle of October, you'll be in for a dazzling display of red, orange, yellow, and purple leaves. Outdoors enthusiasts will enjoy hiking, biking, and fishing at the park. Hunting is also allowed seasonally. The west rim of the canyon is another state park—the Colton Point State Park.

## 160 PINE GROVE FURNACE STATE PARK FREE

**1100 Pine Grove Road**
**Gardners, PA 17324; 717-486-7174**
**advkeen.co/pinegrovefurnace**
***Wheelchair accessible trails. ADA campsites, restroom, and beach.***

Pine Grove Furnace State Park is a narrow park that curves along Mountain Creek. It's hugely popular during summer holidays, with ample space for swimming and picnicking. Fishing, boating, and paddling are all doable at Laurel Lake. The winter months offer space for ice-skating, cross-country skiing, and snowmobiling. One of the highlights of the park is the historic iron furnace that gives the park its name. A section of the Appalachian Trail cuts through the park, and there's a small AT museum on-site. If you are a hunter, there are tons of opportunities at this park. If you are just hiking in the fall or winter, wear blaze orange.

## 161 PRESQUE ISLE STATE PARK FREE

**301 Peninsula Drive**
**Erie, PA 16505; 814-833-7424**
**advkeen.co/presquelslepark**
***Wheelchair accessible trails, visitor center.***

If you want to feel like you are at the ocean without leaving the state, Presque Isle State Park is the place to visit. This park on the shores of Lake Erie is a gem and offers a seemingly endless list of outdoor adventures. Water activities include swimming, boating, fishing, water skiing, and even surfing and SCUBA diving. There are plenty of trails to hike or bike, or you can enjoy lounging on the sandy beaches watching the waves. There are two lighthouses along the shoreline. The Tom

Ridge Environmental Center is at the entrance to the park and is not to be missed. It has great environmental science exhibits where you can learn about the flora and fauna in the park and how to make the most of your visit. Limited hunting is allowed in the park, so check the website for information if visiting in fall or winter.

## 162 PROMISED LAND STATE PARK FREE

**100 Lower Lake Road**
**Greentown, PA 18426; 570-676-3428**
**advkeen.co/promisedlandpark**
***Some accessibility. Contact for details.***

Promised Land State Park is a quiet retreat in the heart of the Pocono Mountains. The two lakes, Promised Land Lake and Lower Lake, are the centerpieces of the park. The land is surrounded by the Delaware State Forest, so you'll be immersed in the natural world. There's plenty of space for fishing and boating adventures, and there are designated areas for swimming in the summer months. The park is in the Pocono Plateau, which means you'll be at a relatively high elevation, but the terrain is mostly flat. Hiking and biking are popular in the park, and winter sports include ice-skating, snowmobiling, and cross-country skiing. Hunting is permitted seasonally.

## 163 RAYSTOWN LAKE FREE

**6993 Seven Points Road**
**Hesston, PA 16647; 888-729-7869**
**raystown.org**
***Varies depending on-site.***

Raystown Lake is the largest lake completely within the state's borders. It's twisty and narrow but spans 32 miles, creating outdoor opportunities throughout Huntingdon County. The lake has abundant water sporting opportunities like boating, paddling, and fishing. Because it's a popular travel destination, there are restaurants and shops throughout the areas surrounding the lake. Land activities include hiking, mountain biking, and seasonal hunting. There are several disc golf courses in the area too. Other popular day trip spots close by include East Broad Top Railroad (see page 92), Lincoln Caverns (see page 125), and Penn's Cave (see page 124). The lake views are gorgeous, so you might just want to plop yourself on the shore and enjoy the view.

## 164 RIDLEY CREEK STATE PARK FREE

**1023 Sycamore Mills Road**
**Media, PA 19063; 610-892-3900**
**advkeen.co/ridleycreekpark**
***Paved, multiuse accessible trail.***
***ADA fishing area.***

Ridley Creek State Park is in a densely populated area, but you wouldn't know that when on the trails, enjoying the natural world. The park is a short drive from Philadelphia, in Delaware County. Rolling hills will greet you along with tranquil Ridley Creek. Hiking is very popular here, as is biking and horseback riding. There are actually two privately run horse farms located within the park. There's lots of space to have a picnic and playgrounds for the littles. You might even stumble upon a wedding, as the park's Hunting Hill Mansion is a popular wedding destination. I'm partial to the trails outside the main park area, particularly the Orange Trail, which offers a quiet walk along the creek. Archery hunting for deer is allowed seasonally, and the park closes one day a year to allow firearm deer hunting. Check the park's website for more information.

## 165 WISSAHICKON VALLEY PARK FREE

**Valley Green Road**
**Philadelphia, PA 19128; 215-685-2172**
**fow.org**
***Forbidden Drive is hard-packed gravel and somewhat wheelchair accessible, although the terrain can be a bit hilly.***

I absolutely love Wissahickon Valley Park. It still never ceases to amaze me that this 2,000-acre forested green space with towering Wissahickon Schist boulders is within city limits. The schist is sparkly, so you'll know it when you see it. The trails are mostly rolling hills, but there's the flatter Forbidden Drive, which is a wide crushed stone path that runs the length of the park. The Wissahickon Creek is the centerpiece, and one of the most beautiful, iconic spots within the park is the Thomas Mill Covered Bridge. The bridge is most easily accessed from the Bells Mill entrance. The park is also wildly popular with mountain bikers, so make sure to listen for bells or voices if you are on a multiuse trail. Shameless plug—if you enjoy hiking, check out my other book, *60 Hikes within 60 Miles: Philadelphia.* There are many featured hikes in the Wissahickon. Hunting is prohibited in the Wissahickon except for occasional controlled deer hunts.

## 166 WORLD'S END STATE PARK FREE

**82 Cabin Bridge Road**
**Forksville, PA 18616; 570-924-3287**
**advkeen.co/worldsendpark**
***Wheelchair accessible picnic area. ADA overlook and cabins.***

World's End State Park is a ruggedly beautiful place. Located in the Northeastern part of the state, there are mountains galore, which means 20 miles of great hiking if you like rocky, steep trails with stellar views. The area called "the rock garden" is a delight to walk through. Towering boulders deposited millions of years ago dot the landscape, providing stunning scenery as you walk through. The Loyalsock Creek runs through the park, and those who enjoy whitewater boating will enjoy rapids from March through May. There's a dammed section of the creek for summer swimming. Winter brings hunters, cross-country skiers, and snowmobilers. If you are an angler, the creek is stocked each year with trout, and the cold waters make good fishing throughout the season. It's close to Rickett's Glen State Park, (see page 129) a waterfall wonderland.

# Pennsylvania Geology, Topography, & Ecology

One of the reasons that Pennsylvania is an outdoor lover's paradise is the varied geology and topography. Much of the state is covered in mountains, which makes for elevation change when hiking or biking. The Appalachian Mountains bisect the state covering large swaths of land from the southcentral to the northeast. There's a small chunk of the Blue Ridge Mountains, more commonly associated with points south. There are also plateaus, which you will often find rolling hills in between. Pennsylvania has the Allegheny Plateau in the west, the Piedmont Plateau in the southeast, and the Pocono Plateau in the Northeast. It's helpful to understand the geology and topography of the state when making outdoor plans, so you aren't surprised if there's a change in elevation.

Most of the rocks in Pennsylvania are sedimentary, meaning they are made from accumulated deposits over time. Shale is the most abundant sedimentary rock in the state, but coal was once a huge industry. Many parts of Pennsylvania were once underneath an ancient ocean that receded to form vast swamplands. Over time, ferns and trees fell and were covered over, eventually to eventually form anthracite coal. Coal is a metamorphic rock, meaning it's undergone some physical and chemical changes over time.

The geology and topography coupled with the state's latitude help determine the ecology. Pennsylvania has several eco-regions, with most of the state covered in a deciduous oak-hickory forest. There's also the northern hardwood forest where you'll see more evergreen hemlock and pine trees. The Great Lakes beech-maple forest is closer to Erie. And there's a small slice of Mesophytic forest in the southeastern corner of the state in Philadelphia and the surrounding counties. Here you'll find trees like sweetgum and southern red oak, more commonly found further south.

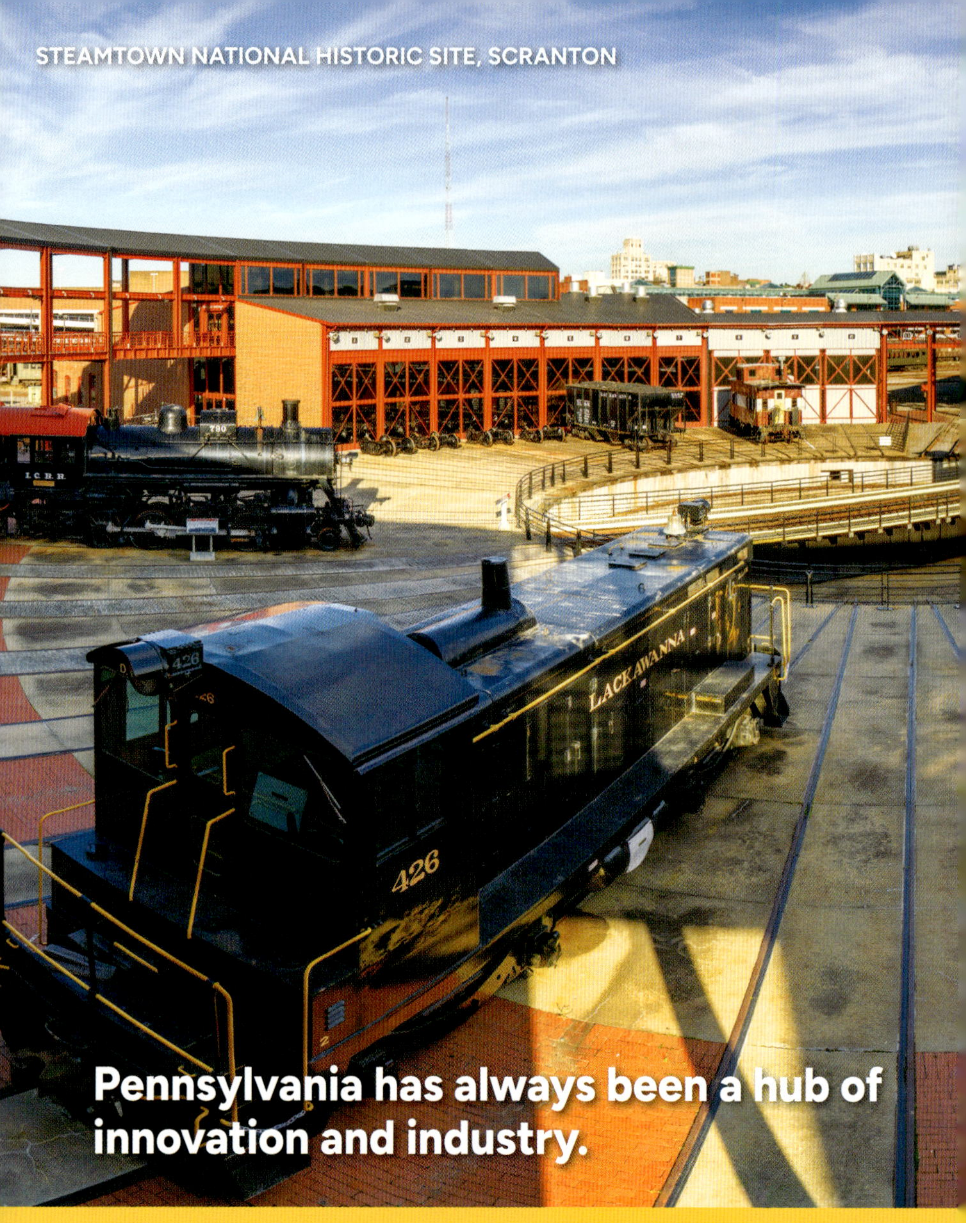


STEAMTOWN NATIONAL HISTORIC SITE, SCRANTON

## Pennsylvania has always been a hub of innovation and industry.

In the 1800s, railroads started popping up in every corner of the state, and industry boomed. The first commercial oil well in the world was in Pennsylvania. Coal, lumber, steel, and iron were big business, cementing the state's place as an industrial powerhouse. The state is rich in preserved history from this industrial time, with tons of places to visit and experience a bygone era. Additionally, check out the "Underground" chapter (see pages 123–125) for coal-related sites.

*Welcome to*

# RAILROADS & INDUSTRY

**Pennsylvania has 65 operational railroads, more than any other state.**

# *Find out more about* RAILROADS & INDUSTRY

## 167 AMERICA'S TRANSPORTATION EXPERIENCE/AACA MUSEUM

**161 Museum Drive**
**Hershey, PA 17033; 717-566-7100**
**aacamuseum.org**
***Wheelchair accessible.***

If you are a lover of cars and car-related history, America's Transportation Experience/AACA Museum in Harrisburg is a great place to check out on a day trip. The museum tells the story of automobiles throughout its 71,000-square-foot space. You'll see a variety of old-timey cars, such as a Tucker auto collection, ranging from the dawn of the automobile to more modern times. In 2020, the museum merged with the Museum of Bus Transportation, so there is a large collection of historic buses that are cool to see up close. For an extra fee, you can even take Model T driving lessons.

## 168 AMERICAN HELICOPTER MUSEUM & EDUCATION CENTER

**1220 American Boulevard**
**West Chester, PA 19380; 610-436-9600**
**helicoptermuseum.org**
***Wheelchair accessible.***

The American Helicopter Museum & Education Center is a unique place that focuses on the history and science of rotary-winged aircraft. It has about 40 real-life helicopters to see up close. Many of the helicopters were used in the military, like the Bell 209 AH-1F Cobra, which served in Vietnam. The museum has an Osprey, one of only a few on display in the world. There are interactive, hands-on exhibits telling the history of helicopters, as well as five interactive aircraft that you can climb aboard and learn about up close. The museum has an education program that focuses on the science and tech behind rotary-winged flight.

## 169 COLEBROOKDALE RAILROAD

**64 South Washington Street**
**Boyertown, PA 19512; 610-367-0200**
**colebrookdalerailroad.com**
***As of publication, the ADA-accessible train car is being restored. Check website or contact ahead of visit to inquire about wheelchair accessibility.***

The Colebrookdale Railroad takes passengers on excursions throughout Berks and Montgomery Counties. The train leaves from Boyertown and travels through an area called the "Secret Valley" along creeks and woodlands. You'll likely see wildlife, such as eagles or deer, on your trip. The train cars are gorgeous and include parlor, lounge, and dining cars. Excursions often include dining and/or drinking, including lunch/brunch, wine tasting, and tea. Themed trips include Valentine's Day, Christmas, and "murder mysteries." The Civil War-era train travels through a historic corridor, passing by a number of iron and industrial sites.

TRAIN ARRIVING AT LEHIGH GORGE SCENIC RAILWAY STATION, JIM THORPE

## 170 EAST BROAD TOP RAILROAD

421 Meadow Street
Rockhill Furnace, PA 17249;
814-447-3285
eastbroadtop.com

***Not all activities are ADA-accessible, but there are some train cars that are wheelchair accessible. Contact beforehand about accessibility needs.***

The East Broad Top Railroad was a lifeline in Central Pennsylvania's industrial past. It hauled tons of coal to the iron furnaces all along its path. Now, it's a National Historic Landmark with a large variety of themed excursions and activities. The steam-powered train has holiday-themed events, food and music events, and many different guided tours. Its focus is sharing the history of railroads in Pennsylvania and across the nation. It has a partnership with the Rockhill Trolley Museum, too, so visitors can buy combo tickets that include a historic trolley ride.

## 171 LEHIGH GORGE SCENIC RAILWAY

1 Susquehanna Street
Jim Thorpe, PA 18229; 570-325-8485
lgsry.com

***Jim Thorpe station is ADA accessible with a chair lift.***

If you are heading to Jim Thorpe (see page 112) and looking for a family-friendly activity, a train ride might be just what you are looking for. The Lehigh Gorge Scenic Railway has diesel-powered trains that take you along the Lehigh River through the beautiful Pocono Mountains. The ride is 16 miles round-trip, but it's a bit shorter in the fall, due to the popularity of its leaf-peeping rides as the surrounding forest puts on a show. Parking is nuts in Jim Thorpe, so give yourself plenty of time to find a spot. The railway also offers bike trips where you can bring your bike and get dropped off in Lehigh Gorge State Park to then bicycle back to Jim Thorpe.

## 172 NATIONAL CANAL MUSEUM

**2750 Hugh Moore Park Road**
**Easton, PA 18042; 610-923-3548**
**canals.org**
***Museum and canal boat rides are wheelchair accessible.***

The National Canal Museum is a hidden gem of a museum that tells the unique history of canals in our industrial past. In the warmer months, you can take a canal boat ride pulled by two mules. Inside the museum are fantastic, hands-on exhibits perfect for young visitors. The museum has a water table, where you can try your hand at building a canal system. It has one major special exhibit each year, focusing on a different theme surrounding the history of the Delaware & Lehigh National Heritage Corridor. There's also a huge park right outside the museum with a playground, picnic pavilion, and walking trails.

## 173 NATIONAL IRON & STEEL HERITAGE MUSEUM

**50 South 1st Avenue**
**Coatesville, PA 19320; 610-384-9282**
**steelmuseum.org**
***Most buildings are wheelchair accessible. Call ahead for accessibility needs.***

Pennsylvania has a deep industrial history surrounding the making of steel. Pennsylvania Steel Company was the first steel maker in the country, and the state is well known for its steel industry. The National Iron & Steel Heritage Museum and grounds tells the story of steel and how it made the state an industrial powerhouse. The 20 acres of grounds surrounding the museum have historic buildings and informational signs throughout. You can grab a brochure for a self-guided tour if you just want to explore outside. If you go into the museum, a guide will tell you more about the history. You can see steel artifacts, including a locomotive and pieces from the World Trade Center's twin towers.

## 174 NATIONAL MUSEUM OF INDUSTRIAL HISTORY

**602 East 2nd Street**
**Bethlehem, PA 18015; 610-694-6644**
**nmih.org**
***Wheelchair accessible.***
***If ASL interpreter needed, please call ahead 30 days before visit.***

The National Museum of Industrial History tells the story of industry across the country. Housed in a repair shop of the former Bethlehem Steel plant, the space is huge and able to display massive machinery. Bethlehem Steel closed in 1995, and the space was reimagined as the SteelStacks Arts & Culture Campus, which revitalized downtown Bethlehem. The museum space features all kinds of industrial machines, many on loan from the Smithsonian's National Museum of American History. In addition to the history of iron and steel, the museum exhibits include information on textiles like silk as well as installations about propane and energy.

## 175 NEW HOPE RAILROAD

**32 West Bridge Street**
**New Hope, PA 18938; 215-862-2332**
**newhoperailroad.com**
***Call to inquire about accessibility options.***

The New Hope Railroad has a variety of excursions that will take you back to a time when railroads were the way of travel. Located in popular New Hope (see pages 113–114), the train travels through the rolling hills of Bucks

County. There are a number of different themed trips, including Valentine's Day trips, wine-and cheese-themed trips, beer tastings, a "speakeasy" trip that will transport you to the 1920s, and Santa trains during the holidays. Close to tons of other sites in Bucks County, including Peddler's Village (see page 114) and the Bucks County Children's Museum (see page 41), it's easy to spend an entire day exploring.

## 176 OIL CREEK STATE PARK FREE

**1080 Petroleum Center Road**
**Oil City, PA 16301; 814-676-5915**
**advkeen.co/oilcreekpark**
***Varies depending on activity.***

Oil isn't the first thing that might pop into your head when you think of Pennsylvania, but it was here that the first commercial oil well was dug. The area is now a state park, where you can explore a bit of history while having outdoor adventures. The Petroleum Center Train Station Visitors Center is where you can learn more about the discovery of oil. There's a huge list of outdoor activities at this park, centered along Oil Creek. There's biking, hiking, fishing, boating, seasonal hunting, and plenty of space for picnicking. The Drake Well Museum (drakewell.org) is nearby if you'd like to learn more about the history of petroleum in Pennsylvania.

RAILROAD MUSEUM OF PENNSYLVANIA, STRASBURG

## 177 PENNSYLVANIA TROLLEY MUSEUM

**1 Electric Way**
**Washington, PA 15301; 724-228-9256**
**pa-trolley.org**
***Wheelchair accessible.***
***Certified Autism Center.***

The Pennsylvania Trolley Museum focuses on the history of trolleys across the state. You can see more than 50 real-life, full-size trolley cars and even take a trolley ride. Santa and the Easter Bunny both stop by seasonally, and the museum has a robust educational program, offering all kinds of programming from field trips and summer camps to STEAM-focused days. It is also a Certified Autism Center, which means that visitors with autism spectrum disorder or sensory challenges can visit during specially designated, sensory-friendly hours. The museum also has a quiet room and sensory bags that guests can request.

## 178 RAILROAD MUSEUM OF PENNSYLVANIA

**300 Gap Road, PA Route 741**
**Strasburg, PA 17579; 717-687-8628**
**rrmuseumpa.org**
***Mostly wheelchair accessible.***
***Call ahead for information.***

If you are a train buff, then you will absolutely love the Railroad Museum of Pennsylvania. Families with little ones who are obsessed with trains will also enjoy the museum. The space is vast, as it houses more than 100 locomotives and other train cars. It's easy to get lost roaming around the vast space. The 2nd floor offers a bird's-eye view of all the train cars below and also has exhibits and artwork. There are artifacts throughout the museum, as well as designated play spaces. Prepare to feel small when standing next to these rail giants.

## 179 STEAMTOWN FREE

350 Cliff Street
Scranton, PA 18503; 570-445-1898
nps.gov/stea
*Mostly wheelchair accessible. Audio descriptions, close-captioning on videos. ASL interpreters available if requested two weeks prior to visit.*

Steamtown is a National Historic Site that's part of the National Park Service. It's a site dedicated to the history and technology of steam railroads and their connection to industrial history. As of the writing of this book, the Visitor Center is closed, but there are plenty of outdoor exhibits to guide your visit. Most visitors come for the train rides. You can take a short trip just for the experience or book an all-day excursion through the Poconos. The "autumn excursions" are popular, as the vast forests in the Pocono Mountains explode into dazzling colors.

## 180 STRASBURG RAILROAD

301 Gap Road
Ronks, PA 17572; 866-725-9666
strasburgrailroad.com
*Not ADA-accessible but call ahead to discuss accommodations.*

Right across the street from the Railroad Museum of Pennsylvania (see page 94), you'll find the Strasburg Railroad. A great day trip might be to spend part of the day at the museum and then head across the street for a train ride. The trips are 30 to 45 minutes, round-trip throughout Pennsylvania Dutch Country. There are numerous themed excursions to choose from for both children and adults, including rides with Santa or the Easter Bunny, escape room adventures, murder mystery rides, as well as lunch-, dinner-, wine-, and whiskey-themed rides. One of the most popular events is the "Day Out with Thomas," led by a full-size, Thomas the Tank Engine™ steam locomotive.

STRASBURG RAILROAD, RONKS

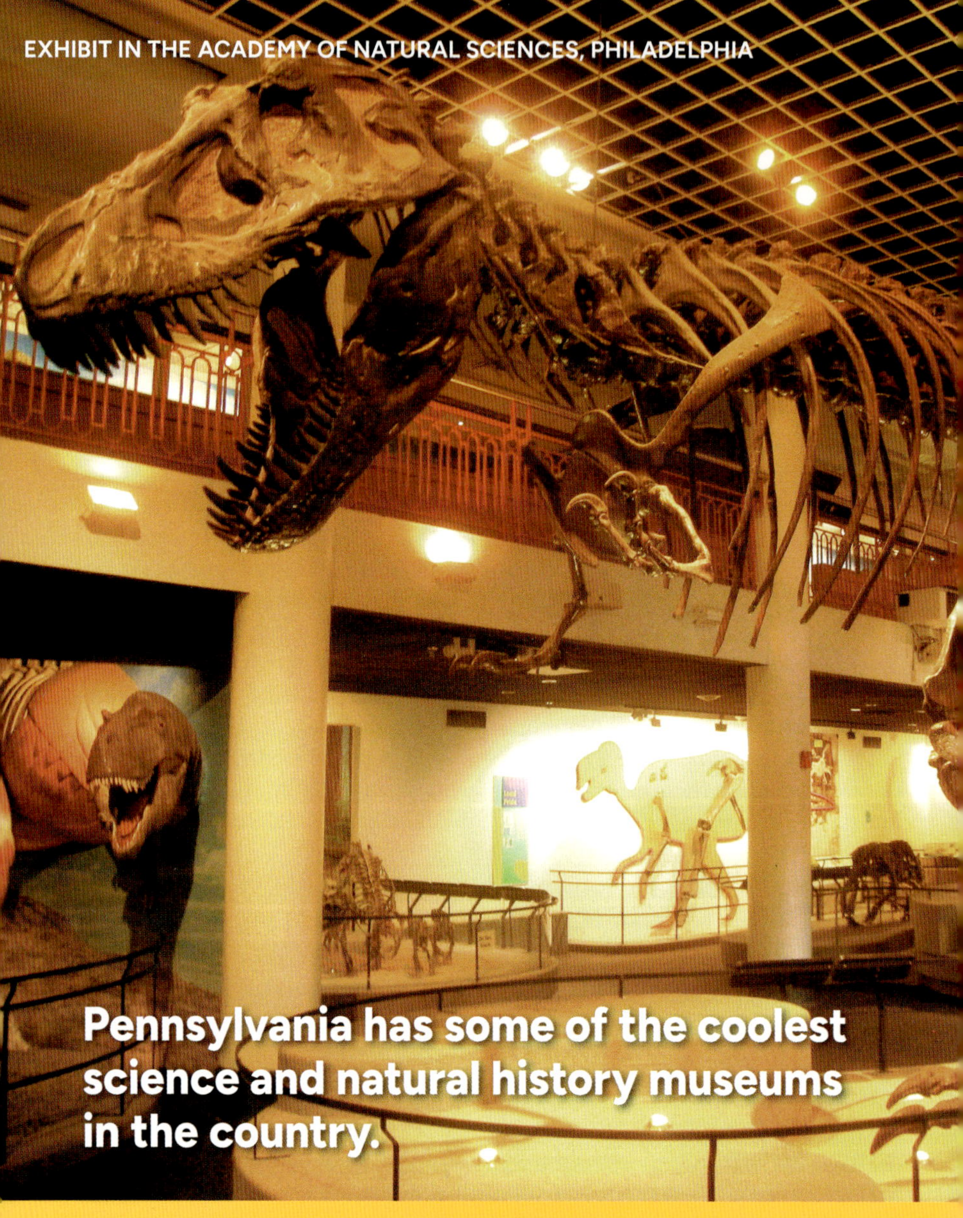

EXHIBIT IN THE ACADEMY OF NATURAL SCIENCES, PHILADELPHIA

## Pennsylvania has some of the coolest science and natural history museums in the country.

Where else can you walk through a gigantic replica of the human heart as if you were a drop of blood? A few of the state's science museums are historic and have been delighting visitors for generations. Others are modern and feature tons of interactive and hands-on exhibits. They are all family-friendly and will no doubt pique the curiosity of young visitors. But these museums are not just for children! Adults alike will enjoy learning about rocks and minerals, flora and fauna, and everything in between.

# *Welcome to* SCIENCE MUSEUMS

*Find out more about*

# SCIENCE MUSEUMS

## 181 ACADEMY OF NATURAL SCIENCES OF DREXEL UNIVERSITY

1900 Benjamin Franklin Parkway
Philadelphia, PA 19103; 215-299-1000
ansp.org
*Wheelchair accessible. Enter through 19th Street entrance. See website for more accessibility details.*

The Academy of Natural Sciences of Drexel University is the oldest natural history museum in the country. If you are looking for a dinosaur museum in the eastern part of the state, this is the place to go. In its Dinosaur Hall, you'll see a towering T-Rex among a variety of other full-size dinos. The Big Dig is popular among the smallest visitors, where they can become paleontologists and dig for fossils. I love the "Outside In" portion of the museum, where visitors can explore animal habitats and maybe even get a chance to touch a live animal. The museum hosts a full calendar of events, including after-hours programs for adults and children.

## 182 CARNEGIE MUSEUM OF NATURAL HISTORY

4400 Forbes Avenue
Pittsburgh, PA 15213; 412-622-3131
carnegiemnh.org
*Wheelchair accessible.*

The Carnegie Museum of Natural History is in a shared space (at no additional cost) with the Carnegie Museum of Art (see page 18). To see both sections in one day is doable, but only if you have a game plan. I'd recommend separate day trips to fully enjoy both parts, but if you've only got one day, make a list of must-see items ahead of time. The Natural History Museum has a fantastic dinosaur exhibit that will make you feel like you've stepped back in time. I'm kind of a rock nerd, so I love exploring the thousands of minerals, gems, and jewels. The Bug Hall is also a favorite spot of mine but won't be for those who are easily creeped out by insects. There's also geology, botany, dioramas, and plenty of life-size wildlife. The American Indian exhibits are stunning.

## 183 CARNEGIE SCIENCE CENTER

One Allegheny Avenue
Pittsburgh, PA 15212; 412-237-3400
carnegiesciencecenter.org
*Fully accessible, including scheduled "sensory sensitive" programming.*

The Carnegie Science Center is all about hands-on learning about the wonderful world of science. There are four floors of immersive exhibits that include ample opportunity for free play. Visitors can build and play in Bricksburgh, learn about water and watersheds, explore a submarine, learn and experience the physics behind sports, and see what it's like to live and work on the International Space Station. There's also a giant cinema where you will feel like you are inside the movie. Plan to spend a full day here and prepare to be tuckered out by the end of your visit.

## 184 DA VINCI SCIENCE CENTER

**815 West Hamilton Street**
**Allentown, PA 18101; 484-664-1002**
**davincisciencecenter.org**
***Wheelchair accessible.***

Allentown's Da Vinci Science Center opened its brand-new home in spring 2024. The center's mission is to get children and families excited about science through immersive, hands-on experiences. Visitors can crawl through a huge intestine and learn about all of the inner workings of the human body. Curiosity Hall is a place where visitors can design and try out their own virtual flying machine, design a self-portrait, and practice being a super-fit kid. The Lehigh River Watershed takes visitors through a limestone cave to meet the center's four resident river otters. Signage is fully bilingual in English and Spanish.

## 185 EVERHART MUSEUM OF NATURAL HISTORY, SCIENCE, & ART

**1901 Mulberry Street**
**Scranton, PA 18510; 570-346-7186**
**everhart-museum.org**
***Wheelchair accessible via rear entrance.***

The Everhart Museum of Natural History, Science, & Art is an eclectic museum located in historic Nay Aug Park in Scranton. In terms of science and natural history, Everhart has fossils and a few dinosaur exhibits, including a stegosaurus. There's also a gallery of rocks and minerals and one showcasing hundreds of birds. The art galleries focus on regional art. Of note are the collection of American folk art and the Dorflinger Glass Gallery. The museum is on the smaller side, so only plan for 1-2 hours. If you visit in warmer months, be sure to stroll through Nay Aug Park and check out the Tree House overlooking a lovely gorge.

## 186 THE FRANKLIN INSTITUTE

**222 North 20th Street**
**Philadelphia, PA 19103; 215-448-1200**
**fi.edu**
***Fully accessible with wheelchair entrances via the 20th Street Business Entrance and the parking garage elevators. Sensory backpacks available to check out.***

It's almost a rite of passage for kids in PA to visit the Franklin Institute. A large statue of the museum's namesake greets visitors who enter from 20th Street. The museum has delighted kids and families for generations. Plan to spend the better part of a day here to experience everything. It's popular and can get crowded, creating teachable moments to practice patience. Things not to miss: the iconic giant heart you can walk through; the planetarium; live science shows; the authentic Baldwin 60000 steam locomotive you can hop aboard; the sports zone; and the 4-story pendulum that swings ever so slightly with the Earth's rotation. And there's so much more than what I've listed. You'll surely be exhausted by the end of your visit.

## 187 NORTH MUSEUM OF NATURE & SCIENCE

**400 College Avenue**
**Lancaster, PA 17603; 717-358-3941**
**northmuseum.org**
***Wheelchair accessible.***

The North Museum of Nature & Science is a gem of a museum. It's on the smaller side, but that makes it very welcoming for pint-size visitors. There are small tables and chairs throughout with many hands-on activities. The Live Animal Room allows visitors to get an up-close look at animals like turtles and snakes. There are exhibits of bugs, birds, bones, and botany. The T-Rex skull is sure to delight anyone with an interest in dinosaurs. There's also a planetarium and an art gallery showcasing regional artists. Even though the museum is small, it's easy to spend a half day here with young children.

## 188 SCIENCE HISTORY INSTITUTE MUSEUM & LIBRARY FREE

**315 Chestnut Street**
**Philadelphia, PA 19106; 215-925-2222**
**sciencehistory.org**
***Wheelchair accessible.***
***Use parking lot entrance on 3rd Street between Chestnut and Market streets.***

The Science History Institute Museum & Library is a lovely little museum nestled in the same neighborhood as Independence Hall (see pages 7–8). It's free to visit and would be a great add-on stop if you are spending the day touring other historic spots. The goal of the museum is to tell stories about the history of science and technology. The museum has artifacts on display in its permanent exhibit along with interactive installations. The museum also has changing exhibits, educational programming, a magazine, and a podcast.

## 189 STATE MUSEUM OF PENNSYLVANIA

**300 North Street**
**Harrisburg, PA 17120; 717-787-4980**
**statemuseumpa.org**
***Fully accessible.***

The State Museum of Pennsylvania is located in Harrisburg, steps away from the Capitol building (see page 10). It has four floors bursting with information and exhibits about Pennsylvania's natural and human history. There's a planetarium with regular programming, a full-scale Mastodon that once roamed the state, and so much more. You could easily spend half of a day exploring and not see everything. I love the Hall of Geology and the exhibit on the formation of coal. There are also exhibits about Pennsylvania's ecology, industry, native peoples, anthropology, archaeology, and the state's connection to the Civil War and Civil Rights movement. If you've got small children, check out the Curiosity Connection, a play space for kids 5 and younger.

## 190 WAGNER FREE INSTITUTE OF SCIENCE FREE

**1700 West Montgomery Avenue**
**Philadelphia, PA 19121; 215-763-6529**
**wagnerfreeinstitute.org**
***Not wheelchair accessible.***

When you step into the Wagner Free Institute of Science, you're entering a museum that has not changed much since the 1800s. It's still mostly arranged as it was when it opened in 1855. There are rows of glass cases with all kinds of specimens, from minerals and rocks to fossils and preserved animals and skeletons. The National Historic Landmark has always been free, as its mission is to provide free science education. The museum has scavenger hunts for first-time visitors, to help you navigate the collections. Wagner also offers classes and workshops. Note: There's no air-conditioning in the building, so I'd make sure to visit on a temperate day.

## 191 WHITAKER CENTER FOR SCIENCE & ARTS

222 Market Street
Harrisburg, PA 17101; 717-214-2787
whitakercenter.org
*Fully accessible.*

The Whitaker Center for Science and Arts is a unique space in Harrisburg that combines a science experience center with a performing arts center, a gaming center, and a huge cinema, all in one place. The UPMC Science Center has tons of hands-on interactive activities that allow children and families to design things, learn about the human body, understand the technology and science behind the making of film and television, learn about the forces of nature, and simply play to learn. The performing arts center has regular live music and theater. Kids can also learn to code and play "purposeful" video games, as well as watch a movie in the cinema space on a four-story screen.

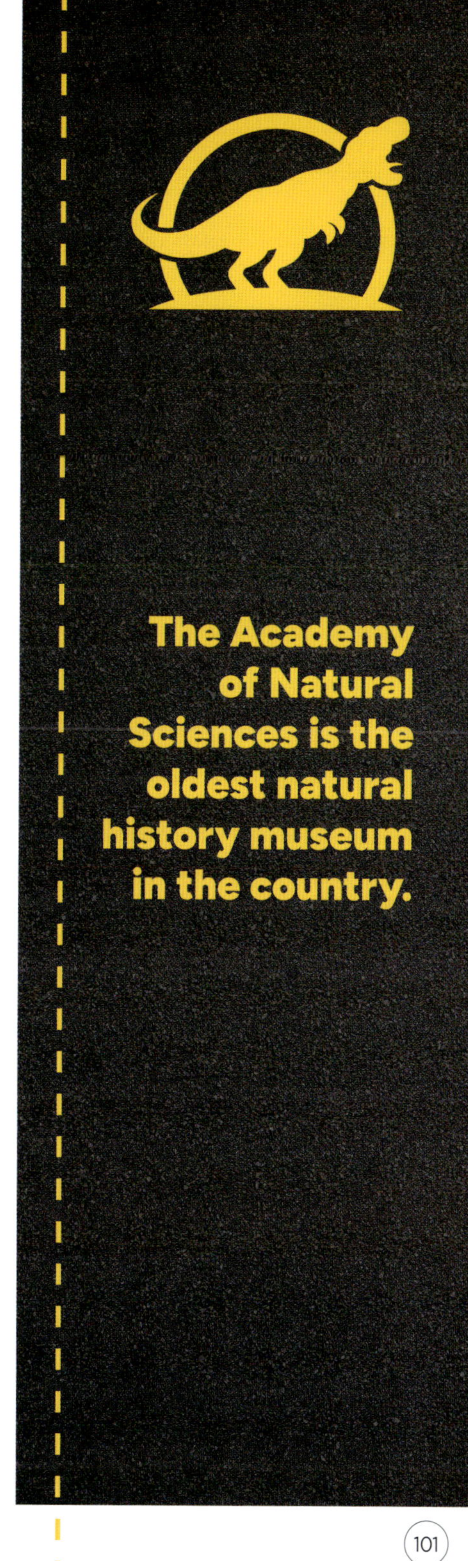

ONE OF MANY SPAS WITH WOODEN SAUNAS IN PENNSYLVANIA.

**I hope you can find some time to take a break and enjoy some of these great self-care spots in Pennsylvania.**

I don't know about you, but I can almost always use a break from stress. Our modern lives are busy and often spent on screens. Stress is so bad for our bodies and minds that we have added a new category to the *Day Trips* series. Personally, I love having outdoor adventures to de-stress, but I welcome time at a spa or lavender farm to breathe and relax. This chapter highlights a few spots across the state where you can spend a few hours or a day just taking care of yourself.

Welcome to

# SELF-CARE

Find out more about

# SELF-CARE

## 192 EVOLVE WELLNESS SPA

**228 South Highland Avenue**
**Pittsburgh, PA 15206; 412-441-0860**
**evolvewellnessspa.com**
***Not wheelchair accessible.***

Evolve Wellness Spa is a quaint and comfy urban spa in the Eastside/Shadyside neighborhood of Pittsburgh. Evolve's focus is on "life-enhancing services," which means you will look and feel amazing after receiving care. The beauty side of the spa will tend to your face's myriad needs. It offers facials, microdermabrasion, and waxing services. I enjoyed an aromatherapy massage at Evolve recently and felt rejuvenated. Evolve has a lengthy massage menu, including relaxation, hot stone, deep tissue, neuromuscular, pre-natal, and craniosacral. Evolve also offers sound baths and massages as well as energy work, like Reiki.

## 193 THE HEALTH CLUB & SPA AT FAIRMONT

**510 Market Street**
**Pittsburgh, PA 15222; 412-773-8800**
**advkeen.co/fairmont**
***Wheelchair accessible.***

The Health Club & Spa at the Fairmont Hotel is a luxury retreat where you will be pampered. Although it is located inside a hotel, the spa is open to the public. Guests can choose from a variety of services, from manicures and pedicures to massages and body treatments. The spa offers couples massages, pre-natal, as well as traditional massages. The hot mud cocoon treatment will fill you with bliss as you are covered in warm mud and wrapped up cozily. Fluffy robes, sandals, cedar saunas, and eucalyptus steam rooms round out the experience. Located in the heart of Pittsburgh's downtown, this spa is perfect for a group party. Light bites are available for purchase.

## 194 HIMALAYAN INSTITUTE & PURE REJUV WELLNESS CENTER

**952 Bethany Turnpike**
**Honesdale, PA 18431; 800-822-4547**
**himalayaninstitute.org**
***Mostly accessible.***
***Wellness Center is fully accessible, as is shrine. Retreat Center main building is mostly accessible.***

The Himalayan Institute & Pure Rejuv Wellness Center is the place to go for a quieter, contemplative self-care day. The institute is mainly a yoga retreat center, but it's easy to spend a day here enjoying some rest and relaxation. The Pure Rejuv Wellness Center is focused on well-being, offering massages and Ayurvedic treatments. Their most popular treatment is Shirodhara, where warm oil is streamed onto your forehead as you relax and enjoy. Enjoy a vegetarian buffet lunch for a suggested donation. Stop by the Sri Vidya Shrine for some silent meditation or take a brisk hike through the institute's trails. To top off your day, stop by Moka Origins (see page 76), which is located on campus, for some coffee, hot cocoa, or delicious chocolate.

## 195 HOPE HILL LAVENDER FARM

2375 Panther Valley Road
Pottsville, PA 17901; 570-617-0851
hopehilllavenderfarm.com
*Partially accessible.*
*Natural outdoor space with uneven ground, but relatively flat.*

A visit to Hope Hill Lavender Farm will no doubt bring you joy and calm. The Pottsville farm is centrally located, and a quick trip from Harrisburg, Allentown, Pennsylvania Dutch Country, or the Pocono region. Purchase a ticket to tour the farm and learn all about lavender plants and their applications in essential oils and cooking. For example, did you know that it takes 11 pounds of lavender flowers to make just one ounce of essential oil? You'll also get to meet the resident farm animals, including horses and donkeys, and get to taste some lavender. You can tour on your own for free during business hours. Don't miss the shop with an array of lavender products, including honey from the farm's bees. The best time to visit is in June or July.

## 196 JOSEPH ANTHONY RETREAT SPA & SALON

### 196A
1200 Market Street, 5th Floor
Philadelphia, PA 19107; 215-310-0036

### 196B
400 West Sproul Road
Springfield, PA 19064; 610-557-0110

### 196C
243 Baltimore Pike
Glen Mills, PA 19342; 610-459-4663
josephanthony.com
*Wheelchair accessible.*

Joseph Anthony Retreat Spa & Salon has three locations to choose from, all offering similar services. Each location has a full-service salon and retreat spa. Enjoy fluffy robes, sandals, a warm foot soak, and complimentary beverages with your visit. I highly recommend booking a soft float treatment, where you will float in what feels like a warm waterbed cocoon. You'll also have time to spend in the brine inhalation room, a quiet space with burbling water, recliners, and blankets. The Center City location also has a sauna and steam room to enjoy along with treatments. The spa will also happily book groups so you can spend the day relaxing with your friends.

## 197 THE LODGE AT WOODLOCH SPA

109 River Birch Lane
Hawley, PA 18428; 570-685-8000
thelodgeatwoodloch.com/spa
*Wheelchair accessible.*

The Lodge at Woodloch Spa is an integral part of this destination spa resort in the heart of the Poconos. Although resort guests get preference, non-guests can check in with the spa two weeks before their visit to purchase a day pass, giving full access to all the spa amenities for the entire day. There are saunas, eucalyptus steam rooms, a snow room, a cold plunge shower, a pool, whirlpools, and amazing water walls that will massage away all of your tension. You can book a treatment separately, but the day pass offerings are expansive, easily filling a day. Enjoy sipping on crystal-infused water and snacking throughout your stay. You can even arrange for lunch and wear your spa robe to dine. The outdoor hot tub overlooking the surrounding woodlands is pure bliss.

## 198 PARADISE LAVENDER FARM

**5822 Paradise Valley Road**
**Cresco, PA 18326; 570-269-8206**
**paradiselavenderfarm.com**
***Partially accessible.***
***Tent area is accessible. Grounds are natural and contain uneven terrain.***

Paradise Lavender Farm is located in the heart of the Poconos. Purchase a ticket to explore fields of lavender. Be sure to take deep breaths of the luxurious smell. In addition to exploring the farm, you can pay a bit extra to pick your own lavender. A special part of this farm is the "Enchanted Fairy Forest," a playground for gnomes and fairies that makes for a lovely "mommy and me" outing. The blooms peak in June and July, but pick-your-own runs through August. This tranquil spot will help you unplug and recharge. Don't miss the gift shop with lavender-themed treats.

## 199 PEACE VALLEY LAVENDER FARM

**802 New Galena Road**
**Doylestown, PA 18901; 215-249-8462**
**peacevalleylavender.com**
***Partially accessible.***
***Sloped ground with gravel spots. Wheelchair ramp to store available upon request.***

Peace Valley Lavender Farm is like a purple beacon on a Bucks County hillside. The farm is close to Peace Valley Nature Center (see pages 25–26), one of my favorite outdoor spots. It is also close to Doylestown shopping (see page 111) and museums like the James A. Michener Art Museum (see page 19) You may find the farm a bit small, but it makes for a great stop on a Bucks County day trip. There is no charge to walk around and delight in the 3,000 lavender plants. Those looking to book group tours should get in contact ahead of time. The space is also leashed-dog-friendly. The gift shop is fantastic and brimming with everything lavender. Bloom time is June and July, but the farm is open year-round.

## 200 RESCUE SPA

**1811 Walnut Street**
**Philadelphia, PA 19103; 866-772-2766**
**rescuespa.com**
***Wheelchair accessible.***

Rescue Spa is a full-service spa and salon located in the upscale Philadelphia neighborhood of Rittenhouse Square. The focus here is about loving and caring for your skin and feeling your most beautiful self. The spa offers hair, makeup, nail, and massage treatments, but its facials are most sought after. There are several facial treatments to choose from, each leaving you looking and feeling years younger. Rescue also offers cutting-edge technology, like LED light therapy, IonixLight treatments, and others, to revitalize your face. The spa offers a full array of top-shelf beauty products to bring home.

## 201 THE SPA AT THE HOTEL HERSHEY

**100 Hotel Road**
**Hershey, PA 17033; 844-330-1797**
**chocolatespa.com**
***Wheelchair accessible.***

The Spa at the Hotel Hershey is also known as the "chocolate spa." Hershey is the chocolate capital of the state, so the spa is close to Hershey Park (see page 42), Chocolate World (see page 74), and Hershey Gardens (see page 52). The spa is located in the Hotel Hershey, which is a delight just to enter. The full-service salon and spa offers hair, makeup, nail, massage, facial, and body treatments. For a bit extra, you can add a hydrotherapy treatment and soak away your worries. I recommend booking a signature cocoa massage, which uses chocolate-scented massage oil. Chocolate indulgence without a single calorie! The spa also has seasonal body treatments invoking the smells and feel of the season. Arrive early and enjoy the sauna, steam room, pool, and whirlpool tub.

PEACE VALLEY LAVENDER FARM, DOYLESTOWN

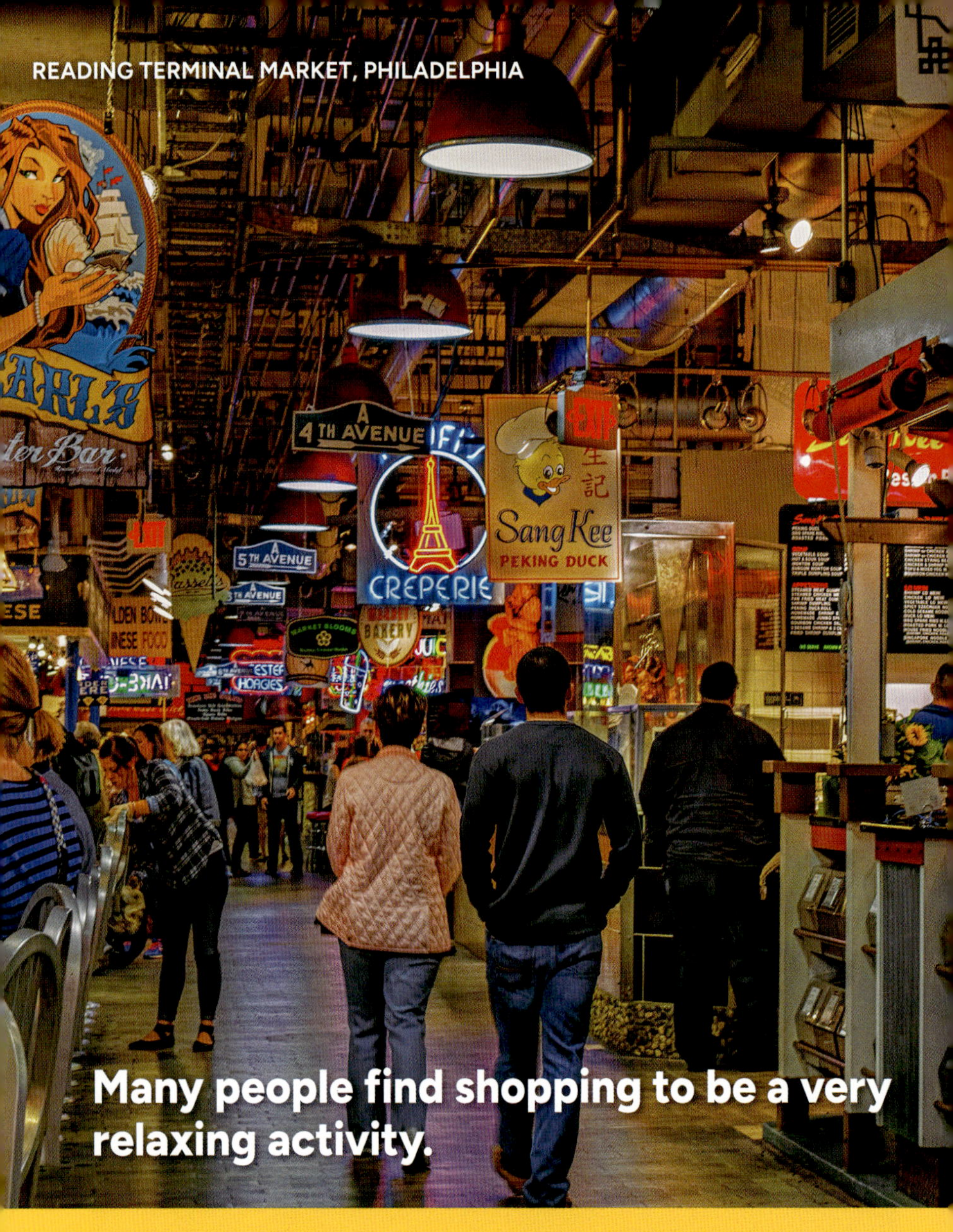


READING TERMINAL MARKET, PHILADELPHIA

## Many people find shopping to be a very relaxing activity.

The term "retail therapy" was coined for a reason! Maybe you are a foodie who loves shopping for the freshest ingredients. Or maybe you like to support small, independent businesses. If so, this list is chock-full of places for you to fuel the local economy. Maybe you are more of a mall person, with everything all in one place. I've got you covered. Since the places in this chapter are near expansive streets, neighborhoods, and markets, I've listed the general geographic area. Aim to start at the center and see what you find. I guarantee you will not be disappointed.

*Welcome to*

# SHOPPING & ANTIQUING

**Pierogies are one of those delicacies you can find in most parts of Pennsylvania.**

## *Find out more about*
# SHOPPING & ANTIQUING

## 202 DOWNTOWN DOYLESTOWN

**Main and State streets**
**doylestownborough.net/pages/shopping**

Doylestown is a ritzy suburb located in Bucks County. The downtown area is where most of the shops are situated, on Main and State Streets, although there are a few on Oakland Avenue There are boutique shops, toys, clothes, home decor, and jewelry shops mixed with great restaurants and bars. I love Doylestown Bookshop (see page 61), which is an independent bookstore with tons of great gifts and games. Doylestown makes for a great daytrip just for shopping, but you can also combine it with museums like the James A. Michener Art Museum (see page 19) or the Mercer Museum (see page 34). It's also close to Peace Valley Nature Center (see pages 25–26) and Peace Valley Lavender Farm (see page 106).

## 203 FRANKFORD AVENUE

**Frankford & Girard Avenues**
**advkeen.co/frankfordgirard**

Philadelphia is such a big city that there are numerous neighborhoods and streets that make for great shopping destinations. Frankford Avenue around the intersection with Girard Avenue is one of those hip neighborhoods that has been up-and-coming for a while. There's a mixture of great vintage shops along with independent, upscale retailers. Harriet's Bookshop is a must-visit for book lovers. You can also shop for plants, home goods, pampered pet supplies, and much more. Great bars and restaurants are interspersed throughout. Parking can be tricky, but you can find a metered spot after a bit of hunting.

## 204 GERMANTOWN AVENUE

**Chestnut Hill, Mount Airy**
**Germantown**
**advkeen.co/germantown**

Germantown Avenue was once a footpath that Indigenous Lenape peoples used. In Philadelphia, it stretches from Chestnut Hill all the way to the Delaware River Wards. The bulk of shopping opportunities are in the upscale Chestnut Hill neighborhood, but great retail has been stretching down the street for years. Neighborhoods like Mount Airy and Germantown also have great shops, especially bakeries, although not as concentrated. You'll find indie gift shops, boutiques, jewelry, furniture stores, kitchen supplies, books, and vintage wares. You can make a day of shopping "the Ave" or combine it with nearby destinations like Morris Arboretum & Gardens (see page 53), Woodmere Art Museum (see page 21), Wissahickon Valley Park (see page 86), or Historic Germantown (see page 7), although I recommend taking a few day trips to explore the area.

## 205 ITALIAN MARKET

**8th, 9th, & 10th Streets from Fitzwater to Wharton streets**
**italianmarketphilly.org**

Foodies should head to the Italian Market in Philadelphia's Bella Vista neighborhood. The parking is tough, but well worth it for the food you will find. Gourmet cheese and meats, along with super-fresh produce, are all available. If you visit for the first time in colder months, don't be startled by the trash can fires; it's all part of the winter ambience. Some of my go-to spots are: Claudio Specialty Foods; Di Bruno Brothers Specialty Foods; Talluto's for amazing homemade pasta; Fante's Kitchen Shop for cookware; and my absolute favorite, Isgro Pastries, which you will smell from a block away. I'd recommend spending a few hours exploring. Go hungry and grab lunch along the way.

FRESH OLIVES AT THE ITALIAN MARKET, PHILADELPHIA

## 206 JIM THORPE

**Broadway and Race streets**
**poconomountains.com/jim-thorpe**

Jim Thorpe is a charming Poconos mountain town with history and amazing architecture. It's a hilly area situated along the beautiful Lehigh River Gorge. Parking is atrocious, so have patience if you are looking for street parking, or just park in a lot. It's walkable, so don't plan to move your car. There are great independent retail stores where you will find antiques, toys, Americana, sporting goods, books, and more. There are also some cafés and restaurants in the shopping district. The Lehigh Gorge Scenic Railway (see page 92) leaves from the center of town, where you can explore the bucolic area via train. It's especially gorgeous in the autumn months when the leaves change color.

## 207 KING OF PRUSSIA MALL

**160 North Gulph Roa**
**King of Prussia, PA 19406**
**simon.com/mall/king-of-prussia**

If you are more of a mall person, head to King of Prussia Mall in Montgomery County. It's the largest mall in the state and the fourth largest in the country. It's difficult to see it all in one day, so I'd browse the website and make a list of stores you want to shop. There are maps everywhere to help you navigate the more than 450 stores. You'll find luxury and international names like Tiffany & Co. and Hermés alongside well-known brands like Bloomingdale's and Nordstrom. There are two food courts and several chain restaurants on-site for refueling. Wear good walking shoes because you'll definitely get in your 10,000 steps.

## 208 LANCASTER & PA DUTCH COUNTRY

**208A Lancaster**
**208B Adamstown**
**208C Bird-in-Hand**
**208D Intercourse**
**208E Ronks**
**208F Lititz**
**208G Ephrata**

Lancaster and the greater Pennsylvania Dutch Country is a popular tourist destination. It's impossible to see all of its offerings in one day. I'd recommend planning a few day trips by town so you can get a good feel for all there is to see. Or you can plan a shopping day where you target certain shops across several towns. You will find Amish and Pennsylvania Dutch foods and desserts, handmade quilts, primitive home decor, Amish furniture, and so much more. There are destination buffet restaurants like Shady Maple Smorgasborg and Miller's Smorgasborg Restaurant. Kitchen Kettle Village is a great cluster of shops. Lancaster's Central Market is a gem. Adamstown has been nicknamed an "antiques capital" of the USA, although I'd argue this entire area is rich in vintage shops.

## 209 LAWRENCEVILLE

**Butler Street from 33rd to 57th**
**visitpittsburgh.com/blog/lawrenceville**

Pittsburgh's Lawrenceville neighborhood has been up-and-coming for a while and seems to have finally arrived. Shops tend to be focused along Butler Street but are also scattered throughout this trendy neighborhood. You'll find shops with art and artisan wares, toys, skincare products, plants, and home decor. The eclectic selection of shops will keep you busy, and there are some delicious restaurants, cafés, and bars along the way to recharge. I find parking to be pretty easy in the neighborhood.

## 210 MAIN STREET, MANAYUNK

**Main Street**
**from Green Lane to Shurs Lane**
**manayunk.com**

Main Street in Manayunk is a bustling street packed with shops, restaurants, and bars. It's situated along a canal that's an offshoot of the Schuylkill River. I love grabbing some ice cream and taking a stroll along the canal towpath with my dog in the early evening. This neighborhood is popular with bicycle enthusiasts, so you'll often see them riding by. Three hundred small businesses call Main Street home and include numerous fitness and wellness destinations, art galleries, boutiques, home decor and vintage shops, restaurants, cafés, and bars. The street also hosts regular festivals where they close the road to traffic, and it explodes with food or art. I'm a huge fan of their annual Arts Festival, which usually happens annually in June.

## 211 NEW HOPE

**North and South Main streets near intersection with Bridge Street**
**visitnewhope.com/shopping**

New Hope is a bohemian town along the Delaware River in Bucks County. Its whimsical shops attract tons of visitors, so parking can be tough but worth it. The tight sidewalks can get crowded on weekends, so be prepared, be patient, and enjoy the vibe. You'll find unique indie shops here with clothes, jewelry, home goods, and antiques. Handcrafted artisanal goods and foods are also well-represented. Many of the restaurants, cafés, and bars have outdoor seating. There are shops off the beaten path, too, and you can walk across the bridge to Lambertville, New Jersey, an equally adorable town.

## 212 PEDDLER'S VILLAGE

**Routes 202 & 263**
**Lahaska, Bucks County, PA, 18931**
**peddlersvillage.com**

Peddler's Village is a destination shopping center, popular with urbanites seeking to get out of cities like New York and Philadelphia. The village vibe is accented by the brick paths and seasonal decor. It gets crowded on weekends and in December. For a quieter, more relaxed shopping experience, consider visiting on a weekday. Artisanal wares and foods are everywhere as well as gift shops and clothing stores. The Lahaska Bookshop (see page 62) is located here and is a must-visit for booklovers. Parking is free, but the lots fill up quickly. Check out the website to peruse the schedule of the many events and festivals Peddler's Village hosts throughout the year.

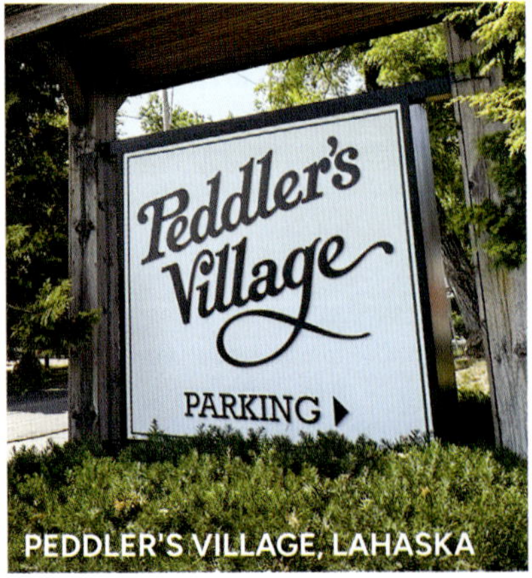

PEDDLER'S VILLAGE, LAHASKA

## 213 PASSYUNK AVENUE

**East Passyunk Avenue from South Broad Street diagonally to South Street**
**advkeen.co/eastpassyunkave**

Passyunk Avenue is a rare diagonal street that bisects the otherwise grid-like South Philadelphia neighborhood. It's hip and trendy and has been for a while. There are many indie shops throughout the neighborhood, where you will find cozy home decor, plants, vintage and collectible items, pet supplies, and toys. A Novel Idea (see page 59) is a great spot for booklovers to visit. Restaurants and popular bars dot the street as well. Parking can be tough depending on which day you visit, but public transit will get you there easily. It's also close to the Italian Market (see page 112).

## 214 READING TERMINAL MARKET

**1136 Arch Street**
**Philadelphia, PA**
**readingterminalmarket.org**

One of the country's oldest public markets, Reading Terminal Market is a foodie's paradise. Centrally located near Philadelphia's Convention Center and City Hall, the market is a popular lunch spot, and it gets packed to the gills. The busy crowds are all part of the experience. Don't get overwhelmed, and do take your time exploring. Go hungry and plan to buy lunch at the endless array of stands. You will have to watch people as you look for a place to sit and eat. It's OK—everybody does it. After lunch, you can pick up fresh produce, meat, seafood, spices, and dessert to take home with you. I've got a sweet tooth, so my favorites include Flying Monkey Bakery, Bassett's Ice Cream, and Mueller Chocolate Company.

## 215 RITTENHOUSE ROW

**Chestnut & Walnut streets near Rittenhouse Square advkeen.co/rittenhouserow**

Rittenhouse Row has undergone changes over the past several years, but it's still a great location to shop. The pandemic affected many stores and restaurants across Center City Philadelphia, but the whole area is trending upward. This shopping area is close to Rittenhouse Square, which is one of the city's original squares. The tree-lined park is a great place to rest, meet friends, or just people-watch. The nearby shopping trends upscale, much like the neighborhood, but you'll also find a great Barnes & Noble. Walnut Street and Chestnut Street are both filled with stores, including the flagship Urban Outfitters. The Shops at Liberty Place are also fun. Great eats abound in the shopping area too.

GLASS CASE WITH VINTAGE FINDS

## Pennsylvania Foods & Food Words

Pennsylvania has several foods for which it is well known. If you are traveling across the state, you will no doubt encounter one or many of these foods. Since food is so intimately connected to culture and language, there are many unique food words that go with these foods. Here are some foods and food words to get you started on your culinary journey.

Cheesesteaks: A cheesesteak consists of thinly sliced or chopped beef on a long roll that is soft on the inside and crusty on the outside. Melted cheese is required, often in the form of Cheese Whiz. You can substitute American or Provolone but don't dare ask for any other kind of cheese. Sauteed onions are optional, indicated by saying "wit" or "witout."

Hoagies: If you are not from Pennsylvania, you may call these sandwiches "subs" or "grinders," but you would be wrong. They are hoagies. Sandwiches on long rolls with a variety of toppings. Whose are better? Wawa's or Scheetz? That depends on which part of the state you live with the West on Team Scheetz and the East on Team Wawa. Central PA has both and Turkey Hill, too.

Lager: A common beer. If you go into a bar and ask for a lager, you will likely be handed a Yuengling (see page 77). If you want a lager by a different name, you need to be specific.

Philly Soft Pretzels: The pretzel was born in Pennsylvania (See Julius Sturgis Pretzels page 74). Anywhere you go in the state, the soft pretzels you find will likely be delicious. A Philly soft pretzel, however, is soft and chewy on the inside, while baked to crusty brown perfection on the outside. They are covered with salt and often dipped in mustard.

Pierogies: Pennsylvania was home to many Polish immigrants who brought with them a variety of their foods. Pierogies are one of those delicacies you can find in most parts of the state. Traditional pierogies are dough-filled pockets of potato and cheese, slathered in butter and caramelized onions. If anyone offers you a pierogi with red sauce, run away as fast as you can.

Shoofly Pie: A decadent Pennsylvania Dutch dessert made with brown sugar and molasses, with a dollop of fresh whipped cream on top. Best found in Lancaster and surrounding towns.

**Scrapple:** Nobody knows what it's really made of, but likely pork scraps and a mish-mash of other things. Often eaten as a breakfast food.

**Water Ice:** An icy, slushy snack, usually made with fruit, mostly available in warmer months. In Philadelphia and parts of Southeastern PA, pronounced, "wooder ice."

**Whoopie Pie/Gob:** A dessert sandwich made of two soft and cakey cookies with sugary cream in the middle. The most common is chocolate cookies with vanilla cream, but I've seen different varieties.

## 216 STRIP DISTRICT

**Smallman Street**
**between 16th & 21st street**
**stripdistrictterminal.com**

Foodies visiting Pittsburgh should add the Strip District to your itinerary. Anchored by the Terminal building and stretching for a square half mile on Smallman Street, "the Strip" is the place to go for hard-to-find groceries, fresh produce, meat, and bread. Visit Pittsburgh calls the Strip "gritty and authentic," and I couldn't agree more. You can also find a Primanti signature sandwich here and enjoy the melty provolone cheese, Italian bread, choice grilled meat, tomatoes, coleslaw, and French fries. The Strip is close to the Senator John Heinz History Center (see page 37) and a perfect place to grab lunch.

## 217 WELLSBORO

**Main Street**
**near Queen Street & Route 6**
**wellsboropa.com/index.php/vacation-wellsboro/shopping2**

Wellsboro is a super-quaint country town, a great place to visit if you are heading to the Grand Canyon of Pennsylvania and Leonard Harrison State Park (see page 84). Most of the shops are clustered along Main Street, but check out the website for a smattering of others off the main drag. Here you'll find sporting goods outfitters and gear suppliers if you are headed on an outdoor adventure. There are also independently owned stores with gifts, artisanal wares, and home decor. If you love games, comics, and puzzles, don't miss Pop's Culture Shoppe.

CITIZENS BANK PARK, PHILLIES, PHILADELPHIA

## From pro teams to college powerhouses, Pennsylvania has sporting events and history for every fan.

Known for its passionate fans, Pennsylvania is home to professional football, basketball, hockey, and baseball teams. In addition to pro sports, the state hosts plenty of amateur and youth events, including the Little League World Series. So, check out a game or two and see some of America's great athletes in action.

*Welcome to*

# SPORTS

## 218 BASEBALL

### 218A Lancaster Stormers–Atlantic League

650 North Prince Street
Lancaster, PA 17603; 717-509-4487
lancasterstormers.com

### 218B York Revolution–Atlantic League

5 Brooks Robinson Way
York, PA 17401; 717-801-4487
yorkrevolution.com

### 218C Washington Wild Things–Frontier League

One Washington Federal Way
Washington, PA 15301; 724-250-9555
washingtonwildthings.com/home/main

### 218D State College Spikes–MLB Draft League

112 Medlar Field at Lubrano Park
University Park, PA 16802; 814-272-1711
mlbdraftleague.com/state-college

### 218E Williamsport Crosscutters–MLB Draft League

Bowman Field, 1700 West 4th Street
Williamsport PA 17701; 570-326-3389
mlbdraftleague.com/williamsport

### 218F Philadelphia Phillies–Major League

1 Citizens Bank Way
Philadelphia, PA 19148; 215-463-1000
mlb.com/Phillies

### 218G Pittsburgh Pirates–Major League

PNC Park, 115 Federal Street
Pittsburgh, PA 15212; 800-289-2827
mlb.com/pirates

### 218H Altoona Curve–Minor League

Peoples Natural Gas Field
1000 Park Avenue,
Altoona, PA 16602; 814-943-5400
milb.com/altoona

### 218 I Erie SeaWolves–Minor League

UPMC Park
831 French Street
Erie, PA, 16501; 814-456-1300
milb.com/erie

### 218J Harrisburg Senators–Minor League

FNB Field
245 Championship Way
Harrisburg, PA 17101; 717-231-4444
milb.com/harrisburg

### 218K Lehigh Valley Iron Pigs–Minor League

Coca-Cola Park
1050 IronPigs Way
Allentown, PA 18109; 610-841-7447
milb.com/lehigh-valley

### 218L Reading Fightin Phils–Minor League

FirstEnergy Stadium
1950 Centre Avenue,
Reading, PA 19605; 610-375-8469
milb.com/reading

### 218M Scranton/Wilkes-Barre RailRiders–Minor League

PNC Field
235 Montage Mountain Road
Moosic, PA 18507; 570-969-2255
milb.com/scranton-wb

**Some of the biggest sports stars have called Pennsylvania home, including Arnold Palmer, Joe Namath, Loretta Claiborne, Lauryn Williams, Kelly Mazzante, and Wilt Chamberlain.**

## 219 BASKETBALL

**Philadelphia 76ers-NBA**
Wells Fargo Center
3601 South Broad Street
Philadelphia, PA 19148; 215-339-7676
nba.com/sixers/

## 220 FOOTBALL

**220A Philadelphia Eagles-NFL**
Lincoln Financial Field, One Lincoln Financial Field Way, Philadelphia, PA 19147, 215-463-5500
philadelphiaeagles.com

**220B Pittsburgh Steelers-NFL**
Acrisure Stadium
100 Art Rooney Avenue
Pittsburgh, PA 15212; 412-323-1200
steelers.com

**220C Pittsburgh Passion-WFA**
ALL AMERICAN+ Field House
1 Racquet Lane
Monroeville, PA 15146; 724-452-9395
pittsburghpassion.com

## 221 HOCKEY

**221A Philadelphia Flyers-NHL**
Wells Fargo Center
3601 South Broad Street
Philadelphia, PA 19148: 215-218-7825
nhl.com/flyers/

**221B Pittsburgh Penguins-NHL**
1001 Fifth Avenue
Pittsburgh, PA 15219; 412-642-1800
nhl.com/penguins

**221C Hershey Bears-Minor League Hockey**
Giant Center
550 Hersheypark Drive
Hershey, PA 17033; 717-508-2327
hersheybears.com

**221D Lehigh Valley Phantoms-Minor League Hockey**
701 Hamilton Street
Allentown, PA 18101; 610-224-4625
phantomshockey.com

**221E** **Reading Royals-Minor League Hockey**

Santander Arena
700 Penn Street
Reading, PA 19602; 610-898-7825
royalshockey.com

**221F** **Wilkes-Barre/Scranton Penguins-Minor League Hockey**

40 Coal Street
Wilkes-Barre, PA 18702; 570-208-7367
wbspenguins.com

## 222 LACROSSE

### Philadelphia Wings-NLL

3601 South Broad Street
Philadelphia, PA 19148; 215-952-5291
wingslax.com

## 223 SOCCER

**223A** **Philadelphia Union-MLS**

Subaru Park
2501 Seaport Drive
Chester, PA 19013; 877-218-6466
philadelphiaunion.com

**223B** **Pittsburgh Riverhounds SC-USL**

Highmark Stadium
510 West Station Square Drive
Pittsburgh, PA 15219; 412-224-4900
riverhounds.com

HE SHOOTS, HE SCORES!

The state was once the coal capital of the country. Today you can venture below the surface to explore former mines. You can also visit natural wonders that were millions of years in the making. Stalagmites and stalactites are mineral deposits that create amazing formations that feel almost other-worldly. Stalagmites grow upwards from cave floors, while stalactites hang down from cave ceilings, and sometimes the two formations even join! If you are looking for a different kind of adventure, maybe it's time to head underground.

*Welcome to*

# UNDERGROUND

## *Find out more about* UNDERGROUND

### 224 CRYSTAL CAVE

**963 Crystal Cave Road**
**Kutztown, PA 19530; 610-683-6765**
**crystalcavepa.com**
***Not wheelchair accessible.***

Crystal Cave calls itself Pennsylvania's first "show cave," meaning it was the first cave that people could visit for fun. In fact, back in the day, people would don their Sunday best for a visit. There was even a wedding there once upon a time. Now, you can visit the underground attraction known for its sparkly underground walls. It's got some very cool stalagmites and stalactites, and the guides spin some lovely tales about the history as you traverse the underground passageways. The temp is 54°F, so it's a great place to escape the summer heat. There's lots to do on-site, including gem panning, picnicking, hiking, and mini golf. Crystal Cave also offers special haunted tours by lanternlight in October.

### 225 ECHO DELL, INDIAN ECHO CAVERNS

**368 Middletown Road**
**Hummelstown, PA 17036; 717-566-8131**
**indianechocaverns.com**
***Not wheelchair accessible.***

If you are looking for a unique, family-friendly adventure, Indian Echo Caverns might fit the bill. Native peoples are believed to have lived in the caverns located near Harrisburg, likely due to the 52°F year-round temperature. The guides are knowledgeable and tell fascinating stories of past visitors. There's a great story about a mystery box discovered in the cave, and its contents are on display inside the shop. The limestone cave formed hundreds of millions of years ago, and the geological formations are stunning. Note: There are many, many steps to get to the cave's entrance, but the walking tour is about 45 minutes of relative even terrain. Outside, there's a playground, gem panning, and friendly animals.

### 226 HISTORIC PENN'S CAVE & WILDLIFE PARK

**222 Penn's Cave Road**
**Centre Hall, PA 16828; 814-364-1664**
**pennscave.com**
***Not wheelchair accessible.***

Penn's Cave is an exciting destination. The cave system is filled with water, so the only way to explore the underground passages is via boat. Be prepared for a steep incline and about 50 steps to and from the dock. The tours last about 45 minutes and take you through the cave channels via a flat-bottomed motorboat. The site also hosts a 90-minute bus tour throughout their 1,600 acres, where you might spy a bison, elk, bighorn sheep, wild horses, or even wolves. Close to Penn State's University Park campus, the National Historic Site has an active calendar of events, including special programming around Halloween and the winter holidays. There's also a maze activity, visitor center, and café.

## 227 LINCOLN CAVERNS & WHISPER ROCKS

**7703 William Penn Highway**
**U.S. Route 22**
**Huntingdon, PA 16652; 814-643-0268**
**lincolncaverns.com**
***Not wheelchair accessible.***

Lincoln Caverns & Whisper Rocks brings together two caves in one tour. A 1-hour interpretive tour leads visitors through the two caverns. Visitors will see sparkly crystal walls and numerous stalagmites and stalactites. This Central-Pennsylvania cave was discovered in 1930 when construction for US Route 22 began. Be prepared to go up and down several flights of stairs with hand railings in the caverns, as well as an uphill walk with more stairs. The site has several events—from black light tours and a bat festival to visits with Santa. Cavern staff love to work with cave enthusiasts, school groups, and scouts. Lincoln Caverns is located near the northwestern section of Raystown Lake (see page 85).

## 228 PENNSYLVANIA ANTHRACITE HERITAGE MUSEUM & LACKAWANNA COAL MINE TOUR

**22 Bald Mountain Road**
**McDade Park**
**Scranton, PA 18504; 570-963-4804**
**anthracitemuseum.org;**
**coalminetournepa.com**
***Museum visitors with special needs should contact the museum ahead of time to discuss accommodations. The mine tour is wheelchair accessible with some restrictions.***

Northeastern PA was once a hub for European immigrants who came to work in the textile mills and mines. The Pennsylvania Anthracite Heritage Museum tells their story. Included in these stories are those who supported the coal industry and came later to the region, including many Spanish speakers. While a separate site, if you'd like to add an underground coal-mine tour to your visit, you can arrange to do so at the Lackawanna Coal Mine Tour. Both sites are in McDade Park in Scranton. The coal mine tour will take you 300 feet belowground to tour an actual anthracite mine. I vividly remember going on this tour with my elementary school and finding it fascinating.

## 229 TOUR-ED MINE & MUSEUM

**748 Bull Creek Road**
**Tarentum, PA 15084; 724-224-4720**
**tour-edmine.com**
***Partially accessible.***

The Tour-Ed Mine & Museum is located about 20 minutes outside Pittsburgh. Visitors will get to experience what coal mining was like. You'll put on a hard hat, get in a coal car, and be guided about 160 feet belowground. Real coal miners are your guides and ensure everyone is safe. The underground portion of the tour lasts about 30 minutes. Back on the surface, the site has a museum with historic mine-related artifacts, as well as a mine rescue vehicle, a sawmill, a strip mine, and a railroad caboose. The picnic pavilion is a great place to eat a packed lunch. The site also hosts a haunted mine event in October.

Waterfalls are abundant across the state, and those listed here are a few of many. The state's glacial past has created fields of giant boulders and gorgeous glacial potholes with water swirling about. Much of Pennsylvania is rural, which also means there is limited light pollution allowing vast, dark, starry skies. We are lucky to have one of the darkest places in the country right here in our state. So prepare to be wowed by what Pennsylvania's outdoors has to offer.

*Welcome to*

# WATERFALLS & NATURAL WONDERS

*Find out more about*

# WATERFALLS & NATURAL WONDERS

## 230 BUSHKILL FALLS

**138 Bushkill Falls Road**
**Bushkill, PA 18324; 888-287-4545**
**visitbushkillfalls.com**
***Not wheelchair accessible.***

Bushkill Falls is actually a series of eight waterfalls surrounded by gorgeous Pocono woodlands. There's a fee to visit the site, but the views are worth it. To see everything, you'll follow a series of trails and bridges. The main waterfall drops about 100 feet. You'll be surrounded by trees, ferns, thick moss, and seasonal wildflowers. The site covers about 300 acres, including 2 miles of trails. The trails are not wheelchair or stroller accessible. There are also extras you can add to your visit, including fishing, picnicking, and a playground. The visitor center has a variety of exhibits, including information about 80 preserved native animals, info about Indigenous peoples, and the history of the falls.

## 231 BUTTERMILK FALLS FREE

**570 Valley Brook Road**
**New Florence, PA 15944**
**724-463-8636**
**indianacountyparks.org/our-parks/buttermilk-falls**
***Not wheelchair accessible.***

Fred Rogers, of *PBS* television fame, was a frequent visitor to Buttermilk Falls. His grandfather, Fred McFeely, once owned the property and used it as his summer estate. Indiana County now owns and manages the site where you can visit the waterfall. Waterfalls tend to be less common in Western Pennsylvania, and although a bit smaller than most, it's still a lovely respite. The park surrounding the falls is about 48 acres and has a hiking trail and small picnic pavilion. Buttermilk Falls is a stop on the Fred Rogers Trail, which is a 10-stop driving tour across the western part of the state.

## 232 CHERRY SPRINGS STATE PARK FREE

**4639 Cherry Springs Road**
**Coudersport, PA 16915; 814-435-1037**
**advkeen.co/cherryspringspark**
***Partially accessible. Call for details.***

It's wild to think that darkness is a natural wonder, but in our modern, well-lit society, it's hard to find a place dark enough to fully enjoy the night sky. Cherry Springs State Park is such a place and is possibly the darkest spot in the eastern US. The park is 82 acres and is surrounded by the vast Susquehannock State Forest. While you can't camp there overnight, you can stargaze all night. If you are a mild night sky enthusiast, consider parking in the public viewing area. But if you've got special gear, like a telescope, you can drive out to the Astronomy Observation Field where you can set up your scopes on one of the many concrete pads. Keep in mind that it gets crowded during celestial events, such as meteor showers, so get there early to secure your spot.

## 233 DINGMANS FALLS FREE

**224 Dingmans Falls Road**
**Dingmans Ferry, PA 18328**
**570-426-2452**
**nps.gov/dewa/planyourvisit/dingmans-creek-trail.htm**
***Wheelchair and stroller accessible to viewing platform.***

Delaware Water Gap National Recreation Area is fortunate to have both the tallest waterfall in the state (see Raymondskill Falls page 131) and the second tallest, Dingmans Falls. Located a short, easy hike from the Dingmans Falls Visitor Center, you'll follow the Dingmans Creek trail for about 0.3 mile to the viewing platform. This section is also wheelchair-and stroller-friendly. If you want to get closer to the falls, the last 0.1 mile is all steps. There's even a bonus waterfall on this trail, and since it's an out-and-back trek, you can see the Silverthread Falls both ways. You'll also enjoy the abundant rhododendrons in the spring and the evergreen hemlock forest surrounding the trail.

## 234 FALLS TRAIL AT RICKETTS GLEN STATE PARK FREE

**695 State Route 487**
**Benton, PA 17814; 570-477-5675**
**advkeen.co/rickettsglenpark**
***Not wheelchair accessible.***

Ricketts Glen State Park is one of my absolute favorite places in Pennsylvania. I spent my high school senior skip day frolicking in the waterfalls. Over a 7.2-mile hike, you can see 21 stunning waterfalls. Be prepared for a difficult hike, ensuring you check the weather ahead of time, wear sturdy footwear, and bring plenty of water and snacks. The Falls Trail is in the Glens Natural Area. If you don't think you can make it through the full hike or are short on time, consider starting at the Lake Rose Trailhead and making an out-and-back trek down to see Ganoga Falls, the tallest waterfall in the park. The website has a great map you can check out to plan your adventure. *Note:* Seasonal hunting is permitted, so if you are visiting during this time, be sure to wear blaze-orange clothing.

## 235 HICKORY RUN STATE PARK BOULDER FIELD FREE

**3 Family Camp Road**
**White Haven, PA 18661**
**272-808-6192**
**advkeen.co/hickoryrunpark**
***Visitors Center is wheelchair accessible.***

BOULDER FIELD AT HICKORY RUN STATE PARK, WHITE HAVEN

Growing up in Northeastern Pennsylvania, I was lucky to have access to so much green space. Hickory Run State Park's Boulder Field was always one of my favorite places to visit. The park itself is gorgeous, but the main attraction here is the 16-acre boulder field you can explore. You can hike out to the field if you are feeling adventurous, but there's also a dirt road you can access with your car. The boulder field is a geological wonder, a remnant from the last ice age full of boulders both massive and small. Hickory Run is huge, so you can easily spend a day at the park. There are 40 miles of hiking trails, cold-water creeks for fishing, swimming in the summer, and snow sports in the winter. *Note:* Seasonal hunting is permitted, so if you are visiting during this time, be sure to wear blaze-orange clothing.

## 236 LAUREL CAVERNS

**1065 Skyline Drive**
**Farmington, PA 15437; 724-438-3003**
**laurelcaverns.com**
***Not accessible. Kaving for Kids simulated cave experience is wheelchair accessible.***

One of the largest caves in the world is in Fayette County. Laurel Caverns is a geological wonder that spans 435 acres underground. It's a sandy limestone cave, home to a large, endangered bat population. But don't worry about coming in contact with the bats—they leave the cave each spring and only return in the winter months when the cave is closed. The cave passages are spacious, with 12-foot-wide trails with high ceilings (between 10 and 50 feet high). A traditional tour lasts about 45 minutes and traverses about 600 feet of relatively easy walking. After the guided portion, visitors are invited to explore on their own by climbing an extra 15 stories to get a truly unique view and experience. If you've got little ones in your group, be sure to check out the Kaving for Kids tour, which is a 10,000-square-foot simulated cave experience meant for children 4 to 8 years of age. There's also gemstone panning aboveground, which is always popular with kids looking for treasures. If you are an adventure lover, Laurel Caverns has some spelunking tours that involve crawling through tight passages and exploring unlit rooms. Kids ages 9 and up can participate in these tours along with an adult. Pennsylvania's governor recently requested that Laurel Caverns become a state park to preserve this amazing ecosystem forever.

## 237 MCCONNELLS MILL STATE PARK FREE

**1761 McConnells Mill Road**
**Portersville, PA 16051**
**724-368-8811**
**advkeen.co/mcconnellsmillpark**
***Handicapped parking available near historic mill. Pavillion is ADA compliant. Contact park for more accessibility info.***

McConnells Mill State Park is a short drive from Pittsburgh. It's gorgeous place, pun intended. The Slippery Rock Creek Gorge creates dramatic rock cliffs and small and tall waterfalls throughout the park. The 19th century gristmill is situated on the banks of the creek. There are a few parking spots at the gristmill, where you can hop out to see whitewater cascading over the falls and then take a walk over the iconic, red, covered bridge. Geology is what makes McConnells Mill special, so if you'd like to learn more, you're in luck—there's a Trail of Geology.

Thousands of years ago, the emptying of glacial lakes created the steep sides of the gorge and uncovered the house-size boulders you'll see everywhere. You can also drive through the park to take in the sights if you aren't interested in exploring on foot or by boat. Park activities include hiking, whitewater boating, picnicking, and rock climbing. *Note:* Seasonal hunting is permitted, so if you are visiting during this time, be sure to wear blaze-orange clothing.

## 238 OHIOPYLE STATE PARK FREE

**124 Main Street**
**Ohiopyle, PA 15470; 724-329-8591**
**advkeen.co/ohiopylepark**
***ADA Accessible observation deck, a rail trail, and cottages.***

Ohiopyle State Park is a popular destination. The rushing Class III/IV rapids of the Youghiogheny River attract whitewater enthusiasts. But you can take in the sights from observation decks near the main parking lot and visitor center. There are also natural waterslides where you can sit in the creek and let the water carry you in Meadow Run. The town surrounding the falls is adorable and has shops and restaurants. The GAP trail also cuts through the park. The park is huge, making it hard to see it all in just one day. The main falls area is the best place to start on your first visit, but I bet you'll be hooked and want to keep going back. *Note:* Seasonal hunting is permitted, so if you are visiting during this time, be sure to wear blaze-orange clothing.

## 239 RAYMONDSKILL FALLS FREE

**983 Raymondskill Road**
**Milford, PA 18337; 570-426-2452**
**advkeen.co/raymondskilltrail**
***Not wheelchair accessible.***

Raymondskill Falls is the tallest waterfall in Pennsylvania. Visitors can find it inside the Delaware Water Gap National Recreation Area. It has three cascades, and when you add them together, the 150-foot drop is just a bit shorter than Niagara Falls. There is an upper and a lower viewing area. The lower is better for photos. The hike to the trail is about a 20-minute walk, but it's steep terrain with an uneven surface. So if you plan to hike, make sure to come prepared. There is a shuttle bus that runs on weekends and holidays from the Milford Knob Trailhead. Overall, this park is huge and has lots to explore, including Dingmans Falls (see page 129), the second tallest in the state.

## 240 RINGING ROCKS COUNTY PARK FREE

**Ringing Rocks Road**
**Upper Black Eddy, PA 18972**
**215-757-0571**
**advkeen.co/ringingrocksparkfive**
***Not wheelchair accessible.***

Ringing Rocks County Park is a great spot to bring kids. Make sure you pack a hammer or two for the trip because the boulders here make music. Nobody knows exactly why the rocks ring, but theories include mineral composition or how they are stacked. The 128-acre park will keep kids busy for a long time. There's also a waterfall in this park, but it doesn't always flow. The best chance to see High Falls flowing is shortly after it's rained. This park is a great spot for a picnic, too, so pack a lunch and spend the day. If you've got children in your traveling group, be sure also to check out the Pocono Environmental Education Center nearby (see page 44).

## 241 SEVEN TUBS RECREATION AREA FREE

**900 Bear Creek Boulevard**
**Wilkes-Barre, PA 18702, 570-945-7133**
**advkeen.co/pinchot**
***Not wheelchair accessible.***

The Seven Tubs Recreation Area used to be a spot only locals knew about. But word has gotten out and the site is hugely popular now, which means the parking lot fills up quickly. The state now manages the site, which is part of the Pinchot State Forest. The scenery is stunning. Glacial meltwater formed the seven potholes ages ago. When I was a kid, visitors would often swim and dive in the pools, which is extremely dangerous and can cause life-threatening injuries. The glacial pools swirl with water, and the water's depth changes constantly. The temptation to wade or jump in is real, but don't do it. There are a few hiking trails at this spot, with abundant wildflowers in spring. The spot has many no-nos—no picnicking, camping, hunting, or swimming.

RIVER STREAM AT SEVEN TUBS RECREATION AREA, WILKES-BARRE

# INDEX

# PHOTO CREDITS

Photos by Lori Litchman except as follows:

Photo taken by **Lori Litchman,** used with permission from **Heinz History Museum:** 28

**Philadelphia Magic Gardens:** 1 (Magic Gardens stairs); **Photo by J. Fusco for VISIT PHILADELPHIA:** 14, 22; **Dave Tavani:** 143; **Photo by R. Kennedy for VISIT PHILADELPHIA:** 108; **Photo by G. Widman for VISIT PHILADELPHIA:** 2

These images are used under CC 1.0 Universal (CC0 1.0) Public Domain Dedication, which can be found at creativecommons.org/publicdomain/zero/1.0/: **Daderot:** 96; **Rj1020:** 42; **Smallbones:** 44

These images are used under Attribution 2.0 Generic (CC BY 2.0) license, which can be found at https://creativecommons.org/licenses/by/2.0/: **ajay_suresh:** 30, no modifications, original image at flickr.com/photos/ajay_suresh/53590379058/; **Nick Amoscato:** 54, flickr.com/photos/namoscato/48468465132/; **GPA Photo Archive-Anthony Quintano:** 46, no modifications, original image at flickr.com/photos/quintanomedia/51858204001/; **Jim, the Photographer:** 40 (Crayola Experience), no modifications, original image at flickr.com/photos/jcapaldi/7297837284/

All images used under license from Shutterstock.com:
**AR54K4 19:** 101; **BK Studio:** 120; **Jon Bilous:** 48; **bioraven:** 90; **Brocreative:** 121; **Cah_You:** 50; **ceoJAHID:** 65; **Dzm1try:** 13; **Zack Frank:** 88; **Irina Gutyryak:** i (asphalt); **il21:** 70; **JosepPerianes:** 27; **Kat Giannikos Photography:** 133; **Kavic.C:** 87; **Life Atlas Photography:** 36; **Masum411:** 80; **MH Anderson Photography:** 129; **Mr. Tempter:** 102; **OMIA silhouettes:** 11; **PCAStudio-1:** i (liberty bell); **Hope Phillips:** 112; **Zachary Chung Pun:** i (Shofuso Japanese House); **RajaDigital:** 16; **Michael Ridall:** xvi (Cherry Springs Park); **Victoria Sergeeva:** 110; **Shamanistik:** 77; **Soft_Light_Studio:** 75; **Thu Lai Photography:** 92; **Tuesday04:** 40 (crayon art); **Buzaeva Valeriia:** 67; **Vershinin89:** 68; **Tatyana V. Vorontsova:** 117

# ABOUT THE AUTHOR

**Lori Litchman** is a lifelong Pennsylvanian, growing up in the Pocono Mountains and then settling in Philadelphia. She is the author of *60 Hikes within 60 Miles: Philadelphia.* She's an avid hiker who loves exploring snowy meadows and mossy forests with her husband. She's also certified as a Level 1 Mindful Outdoor Leader and enjoys connecting others to the more-than-human world. Check out her websites: phillyhiking.com and pennsylvaniadaytrips.com.

**The Story of AdventureKEEN**

We are an independent nature and outdoor activity publisher. Our founding dates back more than 40 years, guided then and now by our love of being in the woods and on the water, by our passion for reading and books, and by the sense of wonder and discovery made possible by spending time recreating outdoors in beautiful places.

It is our mission to share that wonder and fun with our readers, especially with those who haven't yet experienced all the physical and mental health benefits that nature and outdoor activity can bring.

In addition, we strive to teach about responsible recreation so that the natural resources and habitats we cherish and rely upon will be available for future generations.

We are a small team deeply rooted in the places where we live and work. We have been shaped by our communities of origin—primarily Birmingham, Alabama; Cincinnati, Ohio; and the northern suburbs of Minneapolis, Minnesota. Drawing on the decades of experience of our staff and our awareness of the industry, the marketplace, and the world at large, we have shaped a unique vision and mission for a company that serves our readers and authors.

**We hope to meet you out on the trail someday.**

**#bewellbeoutdoors**